"Joy's biblical and practical examples of the working of the Holy Spirit are inspiring and truly offer hope to anyone who believes in the power of God to unify the body of Christ. The tone of humility with which Joy penned this work is a wonderful example to us all."

—Vonette Bright, co-founder, Campus Crusade for Christ (now Cru in the United States)

"Joy Dawson is a gifted master-teacher and prophetic voice. In a very real and dynamic sense, this book has been given to her as a 'word from heaven' and should shake us up to act upon it. It has shaken me anew."

—from the foreword by Jack Hayford, chancellor, The King's University; founding pastor, The Church On The Way

"Joy Dawson (Mom, to me) has given us, possibly, her most important book because it gets to the heart of what ails us as Christians and presents the solution."

—from the foreword by John Dawson, founder, International Reconciliation Coalition; international president emeritus, Youth With A Mission

HEAVEN
WILL
BREAK LOOSE

All
HEAVEN
WILL
BREAK LOOSE

When We Make *the* Priorities of
Jesus Our Pursuit

JOY DAWSON

Chosen

a division of Baker Publishing Group
Minneapolis, Minnesota

Published by Chosen Books
11400 Hampshire Avenue South
Bloomington, Minnesota 55438
www.chosenbooks.com

Chosen Books is a division of
Baker Publishing Group, Grand Rapids, Michigan

Printed in the United States of America

Library of Congress Cataloging-in-Publication Data is on file at the Library of Congress, Washington, DC.

ISBN 978-0-8007-9582-5 (pbk.)

Every effort has been made to identify the source of the song lyrics quoted in chapter 8 ("Lost sinners are dying in darkness today . . ."). Chosen Books welcomes any information that would allow us to give proper credit to the songwriter.

Unless otherwise indicated, Scripture quotations are from the New King James Version. Copyright © 1982 by Thomas Nelson, Inc. Used by permission. All rights reserved.

Scripture quotations identified ESV are from The Holy Bible, English Standard Version® (ESV®), copyright © 2001 by Crossway, a publishing ministry of Good News Publishers. Used by permission. All rights reserved. ESV Text Edition: 2007

Scripture quotations identified NIV are from the Holy Bible, New International Version®. NIV®. Copyright © 1973, 1978, 1984, 2011 by Biblica, Inc.™ Used by permission of Zondervan. All rights reserved worldwide. www.zondervan.com

Scripture identified NIV1984 taken from the HOLY BIBLE, NEW INTERNATIONAL VERSION®. Copyright © 1973, 1978, 1984 Biblica. Used by permission of Zondervan. All rights reserved.

Scripture quotations identified RSV are from the Revised Standard Version of the Bible, copyright 1952 [2nd edition, 1971] by the Division of Christian Education of the National Council of the Churches of Christ in the United States of America. Used by permission. All rights reserved.

Scripture quotations identified KJV are from the King James Version of the Bible.

Cover design by Gearbox

13 14 15 16 17 18 19   7 6 5 4 3 2 1

Dedication

I am dedicating this book to my dear son, John, the
founder of the International Reconciliation Coalition.
This movement, under God's mighty hand, has been and
still is an enormous catalyst in uniting people groups
globally who were/are divided. It was founvded in 1990.

I want to honor John for being willing to pay the price
of being a broken vessel in the Master Potter's hand
to spearhead one of the most significant movements
in our time that directly relates to Jesus' prayer in
John 17:21, "that they all may be one, as You, Father,
are in Me, and I in You; that they also may be one in
Us, that the world may believe that You sent Me."

I long for this book to encourage him, as his vital
ministries have encouraged mine. John is the international
president emeritus of Youth With A Mission.

Contents

Foreword

Joy Dawson (Mom, to me) has given us, possibly, her most important book because it gets to the heart of what ails us as Christians and presents the solution. I am delighted and encouraged.

I have served a variety of networks and movements around the world, most recently as the president of Youth With A Mission. Bitter experience has taught me that the greatest plans and projects fail when our hearts are divided, including the greatest project of all, completing the Great Commission.

Just last week, Paul Eshleman, a global leader whom we associate with the *JESUS* film, spoke to a large assemblage of leaders on the subject of unity. He said, "We have promoted the resurrection as the apologetic for Jesus being the Son of God. However, John 17 reveals that it is the loving unity of His followers."

This is a new day. Pioneers such as David du Plessis paid a price to lead us out of the wilderness of sectarian division. Today it is more common to see movements and denominations functioning as complementary parts of the whole, rather than as reactive, exclusive and separate. Count Zinzendorf's dream of Christian unity has come to fruition in some measure. We remain vulnerable, however, to the spirit of religious controversy and the pride of leadership. Jesus, help us.

I am deeply grateful for the example of my parents, both for the harmony of their marriage of 65 years and for the integrity with which they have stewarded great influence during that time. They have lived this book, and if we do the same, all heaven will break loose.

—John Dawson

Foreword

It was confirmed by a small earthquake. I will never forget the day!

A dozen of the Los Angeles area's leading pastors had gathered, each an independent thinker, but also with clear-eyed commitment to the Word of God and the testimony of Jesus Christ. Each had accepted my invitation to breakfast, each was from a different sector of the evangelical community and all were men with fruitful ministries. The Holy Spirit had moved me to call them together to join with me in seeking to band together as many pastors in the greater city as possible into a teamed prayer-force.

Following breakfast, I related the specifics of my sense of assignment—an assignment I knew could never be fulfilled without a group of pastors from varied sectors of Los Angeles' cosmopolitan mosaic, ethnically, theologically and socially. The most direct approach required a risk of my being misunderstood, but I decided to take it. I related to the brethren how the Lord had awakened me one morning three months before and had said, "Pray against the destruction of the city of Los Angeles."

I told them how I had laughed—not at God or in mockery of His "word" to my heart, but at myself. I knew it was the Lord and I knew I would obey, but at the same moment I recalled the number of times "prophets" had announced our city's destruction at appointed dates—and then nothing had happened. I thought, *Maybe this is how all those guys began!* But I went on to say to the leaders gathered with me, "Thank you for trusting me enough to hear me out. I want to submit to your counsel on this."

I then related three things:

- First, I explained that on the morning the Lord had impressed me with this call to prayer, as I waited on Him, the Holy Spirit gave *immediate* focus: "I am not referring to the future of Los Angeles. Los Angeles *is being destroyed right now!*" I was deeply stirred, drawn to pray against the societal and physiological afflictions that were/are "destroying" marriages, physical bodies, businesses, children, minds, hopes and dreams. (Projections at the time—that thousands would die that year from various terminal diseases—added significantly to the "destruction" warning I received from God's heart.)

- Second, I related my concern over a recent article in the *Los Angeles Times*. It relayed the report of a group of seismologists who, having met, outlined for L.A.'s emergency agencies a scenario of the first four days following a 7.0 quake, centered on the line of a fault that runs through downtown to the west, at five o'clock on any given workday. The report unfolded how the number dead from the multiple impact of destruction, fires and the mobility limits of emergency agencies in the aftermath would be over twenty thousand. Shattered water mains, as well as general upheaval, would leave fires burning for at least four to seven days. The situation was unimaginably disturbing.

- Third, having made clear that a dramatic natural disaster was not the sole issue, and that God's call was to "pray against the destruction of the city of Los Angeles," I proceeded to share with these leaders my sense of the need that we unify our leadership, call the pastors together and by our model to unite, give a clear signal that "the whole church that believes prayer can change the city" move forward toward such prayer.

I finished my post-breakfast remarks and said, "So, brothers, that's why I asked you to come today—thank you for hearing me out."

There was a silence for no more than three seconds, and then an earthquake occurred!

It was only about a 2.0 table and window shaker, and it only lasted for about five seconds. But it was as dramatic a moment as I have ever known. We were all struck with the stark reality of the issue and a deep sobriety. Then we relaxed and looked around at each other.

One of the men said, "I think we know what we're supposed to do!"

There was a mix of relieved laughter, but also an instantaneous agreement and introductory bonding to take our places, unite and use our leadership to call Los Angeles' pastors to come together in prayer—no matter what Christian denomination or affiliation they represented. The story goes on . . . and it did, three times a year for seven years, with an average of at least five hundred pastors assembled for passionate prayer, worship and intercession. We called it "LOVE L.A. and PRAY," and when pastors returned to their flocks and reported our unity, hosts of congregations awakened to new levels of prayer!

I only tell this story as a foreword to Joy Dawson's book because I believe this:

- It illustrates the desire of God's heart to signal earnest believers when an hour of greatest need is at hand—one calling us to *overcome separatism and unite in prayer*.
- It exemplifies the fact that believers *can* and *will* be awakened to unity and intercession if they are jolted by a God-given wake-up call; and *this book is one!*

Three more things in conclusion. First, we need to pray against the destruction of cities and nations—and to allow the fiery passion of the Holy Spirit to move us with the awareness that *they are being destroyed*. As we speak, this moment, our adversary the destroyer is at work.

Second, we will be blessed to be *moved* by what I believe is a "word from heaven" contained in this book. Joy Dawson (who, incidentally, attended many of those LOVE L.A. prayer meetings when she was in the city) is a gifted master teacher and prophetic voice—especially when the subject of prayer is on the table.

Third, in a very real and dynamic sense, I believe this book has been given to Joy to relay to us at this time as an *earthquake truth*—and as enough of a shake-up to bring us to decision. It is a weighty moment across the face of our earth, a violently destructive era in many nations and a literal "hell-bent" season in city after city and region after region. It is desperately so in my homeland, America.

I have been touched by *All Heaven Will Break Loose*! It has shaken me anew. A real shake-up will cause anyone to join hands with anyone they can. It is time for the whole Church to be shaken enough to join hands. The earth is shaking.

—Pastor Jack Hayford

Acknowledgments

Always first is my enormous gratitude to God for His amazing grace that enabled me to write this book under difficult physical circumstances.

I am also deeply grateful to my beloved husband, Jim, for his many prayers, his helpful input when I would ask questions and his releasing me to prioritize my time on this project, which meant that he had to take a heavier load in other areas. He did so without complaint. At 90 years of age, on February 24, 2013, he went to be with his Lord and Master. We were life partners and sweethearts for 65 years.

Then there is precious Jessica Hover, from YWAM Los Angeles staff, who took all my handwritten scripts and put them into a computer for this project. She was an incredible gift from God— humble, conscientious, skillful and a delight to partner with.

I was only able to contact a small number of my intercessor friends to ask for their prayer support for this project. I pray that God will greatly reward and uniquely bless them for their faithfulness. How I needed those prayers!

I also want to express my deep gratitude to my dear friend Jane Campbell for her prayers and for helping me navigate all the publishing ramifications.

1

When Leaders Lead
in God's Priorities

It was a Sunday morning service at our Baptist church when we used to live in Auckland, New Zealand. Our pastor, the Reverend Hayes Lloyd, was coming near to the close of the service when he announced with obvious strength of conviction, "That's the end of the message, but it's not the end of the service."

Immediately I whispered to my husband, Jim, "This must be it!" All week long, while in intercession for my pastor, the Holy Spirit had been revealing to me that God was going to require of him that he do something difficult on Sunday morning. The purpose was so that I would pray for God's enabling grace and power to be upon him to discharge it fully—whatever it was. I did just that in faith, fervently and frequently.

With a God-given boldness devoid of the fear of men, the pastor said these historic words: "*Let's rip up the labels*—the labels that divide the Body of Christ, and us as a church."

He enumerated some of them—"Evangelicals, Pentecostals, charismatics, Armenians, Calvinists, Baptists, Lutherans, Roman Catholics, Presbyterians, Methodists, Anglicans—pre-Trib/post-Trib and any and every other label that divides us in heart. Our diversity is obvious, but is it our primary identity? Let's rip up the secondary labels that have been lifted too high and simply be known as Christians—Christ's ones when we speak to the world."

Then he called everyone to repent before God of the sins of pride and prejudice where we were not in unity. He made no suggestions and gave no orders as to how we were to do that. God alone knew each person's history and attitudes toward other parts of the Body of Christ.

I remember immediately seeing men prostrate, facedown on the floor, underneath the pulpit and in the aisle, weeping before God. Many were kneeling with heads bowed in deep repentance as the Holy Spirit swept into that church and over God's people. This pastor, a former president of the Baptist Union in New Zealand, was used of God to unite that congregation at a time when evangelicals struggled with renewal movements during the 1960s. He led the congregation in fearing and obeying God related to unity. This led to a whole new moving of the Spirit among us that affected every part of church life, including an ingathering of previously alienated people.

Oh, how we need God-fearing spiritual leaders today who will stand up and call God's people to unite in every nation, in the interests of living by God's standards of righteousness from His holy Word. Jesus stated it clearly and simply in Matthew 12:25: "Every kingdom divided against itself is brought to desolation, and every city or house divided against itself will not stand."

When two newlyweds were arguing with one another, the wife lifted up her left hand and pointed to her wedding ring. She said, "Remember? We're both on the same team!"

As Bishop John Garlington once said, "We sometimes sing the song, 'Blessed Be the Tie That Binds Our Hearts in Christian Love.' Sadly, we often can't see the tie because of the knots."

We may need to be reminded that if Jesus Christ is our Lord and Master, and if we are trusting in His completed work on the cross as our only means for the forgiveness of our sins and for obtaining eternal life, then . . .

We Are All on the Same Team

We've all got the same Father—God.

We've all got the same Savior—Jesus.

We've all got the same Empowerer—the Holy Spirit.

We've all got the same Textbook—the Bible.

We've all got the same enemy—the devil.

We've all got the same orders—the Great Commission.

We've all got the same promise—*"I am with you always."*

We've all got the same destination—heaven.

We've all got the same assignment—to bring heaven's blessings to earth.

Let's wise up and understand that because we all will spend the endless ages of eternity together, we had better get used to the idea and start enjoying the unity that, four times in John 17, Jesus prayed to the Father we would have. After all, God answers Jesus' prayers, because the Trinity is in perfect unity. Therefore, Jesus means us to believe that His prayer in John 17:23 is that we may experience this kind of unity—Trinity unity—here on earth: "I in them and you in me. May they be brought to complete unity to let the world know that you sent me and have loved them even as you have loved me" (NIV1984).

Amazing! Incredibly wonderful! Doable! Purposeful!

God has varied ways of using spiritual leaders to bring unity. He is never in a mold. And those who are totally yielded to the Holy Spirit's moving find that He is never predictable. When spiritual leaders have really made the decision to at all times become nothing that God may be everything . . . then anything can happen.

That kind of "anything" inevitably brings glory to Jesus, not man. In John 17:22, when Jesus is praying for unity among all His disciples, He links His glory with the request: "And the glory which You gave Me I have given them, that they may be one just as We are one."

While writing this book, my husband and I saw up close a beautiful example of a spiritual leader living what I am talking about. It was nearing the end of the 11:00 a.m. Sunday church service. Our lead pastor, Dr. Ricky Temple, was sharing from his heart about the need for us as the people of The Church On The Way to be more involved with meeting the great needs of the poor and needy around us. He said he would love for us to have a place on the outside of one of our buildings where the homeless could come at any time and take a shower . . . as just one example.

Pastor Ricky went on to say how awful the circumstances are and how desperate are the needs of people outside the walls of our church . . . and how he longs to reach them with the Gospel, in the ways that Jesus did. Then he stopped, dropped his head, covered his face with his hands and wept. He asked our senior executive pastor to conclude the service, which he immediately did while Pastor Ricky sat down on the front row, still deeply impacted by the Holy Spirit with a burdened heart for suffering, lost people.

The effect on the congregation was powerfully unifying. Many caught what the Holy Spirit was saying and doing. We heartily clapped our hands in full approval. Some stood, waving their hands above their heads, trying to express their wholehearted response. Our pastor had paid a price to share God's heart. As a congregation we badly wanted to communicate to him, "We are one with you in spirit. We will do whatever God shows us. Keep leading us, dear man of God."

I am so thankful that James Robison, a Baptist, and Jay Richards, a Catholic, have together sent out a clear clarion call for all believers to take a firm stand for this unity for which Jesus prayed. The following excerpts are taken from their excellent book *Indivisible* (FaithWords, 2012).

> We need to go beyond defensive alliances on public policy . . . and strive for a deeper and more lasting unity. We have serious doctrinal disagreements, but we share core beliefs and moral principles and worship the same God.
>
> In the last couple of years, the two of us . . . have met with scores of Catholic and Protestant leaders and spoken to thousands of Christians around the U.S.A. . . . Over and over, we have heard the same thing: The Holy Spirit seems to be drawing together all of those in the Judeo-Christian tradition despite our differences. We're convinced that God wants to pour out His Spirit on the Church for the good of our entire culture.
>
> Oneness is not sameness. In fact, diversity grounded in unity can be an asset. . . .
>
> If we are to be salt and light for our culture, we must be able to understand and explain the sources of darkness with a consistent voice.

That is just "the tip of the iceberg" of what I believe is an historic and timely book.

Satanic forces know their time is short before the Second Coming of our Lord and Savior, Jesus Christ. "Therefore rejoice, you heavens and you who dwell in them! But woe to the earth and the sea, because the devil has gone down to you! He is filled with fury, because he knows that his time is short" (Revelation 12:12

NIV). Consequently, his forces have united to spew out the vilest and most heinous plans to destroy the lives of humanity—especially the most helpless and defenseless among us.

The sex-trafficking of innocent little children, who are kidnapped and then forced to perform the vilest acts of sexual perversion, is beyond anything we could have imagined. The Bible has warned us, "The thief [Satan] does not come except to steal, and to kill, and to destroy" (John 10:10).

I am deeply convinced that we as believers should be united in crying out to God in faith-filled prayers that He would rescue these precious little ones from this hellish life. My husband, Jim, and I did that for years, and it is high on my priority of intercessory prayer projects.

God links together those who have knowledge of His character with those who are helping the helpless. "'He judged [defended] the cause of the poor and needy; then it was well. Was not this knowing Me?' says the LORD" (Jeremiah 22:16).

Predators stalk the villages up in the mountain areas of Nepal, where food is very scarce, and kidnap little children. They promise these children food and a good life, and then, to gratify their own sexual perversions, they lock these little ones up and treat them far worse than animals. I hear God calling His people to get desperate in intercession because of these heinous practices. Look at Jeremiah 9:20–21:

> Yet hear the word of the LORD, O women, and let your ear receive the word of His mouth; teach your daughters wailing, and everyone her neighbor a lamentation. For death has come through our windows, has entered our palaces, to kill off the children—no longer to be outside!

It is reported that sex trafficking makes up a surprisingly large part of the global economy. How shocking is that! How God's heart must break for these precious children who were all made in His image. Jesus said in Matthew 18:6, "Whoever causes one of these little ones who believe in me to sin, it would be better for him if a millstone were hung around his neck, and he were drowned in the depth of the sea." The New International Version (1984) translation of a verse that follows closely is significant. It says, "See that you do not look down on one of these little ones. For I tell you that their angels in heaven always see the face of my Father in heaven" (verse 10). That means the angels are on the alert, looking at God and ready to move at a moment's notice at His direction on behalf of those little ones. And we can either be involved in faith, interceding for God to activate the angels to rescue them, or be unconcerned and indifferent, thinking we have more important things to do.

Jesus warns against that.

God has many ways of rescuing these helpless little ones and putting them in loving Christian orphanages and homes. Also, that horrendous warning from verse 6 comes from the loving heart of God that breaks over the inevitable judgment coming to those who force children into sexual abuse. In the place of intercession, the Holy Spirit burdened Jim's heart and mine for these men and gave us faith to believe for a sweeping wave of spiritual awakening that will reach them when nothing else can. God has done it before. Thousands of Christian workers and social activists are working on the problem, and believers everywhere need to join and support them, but progress has been agonizingly slow. The world needs a spiritual breakthrough that will release social transformation.

Genuine Revival

The following is an adaption of quotations from Andrew A. Woolsey's *Channel of Revival: Biography of Duncan Campbell* (Faith Mission, 1982), who was mightily used of God in the

Hebrides Islands revival off the coast of Scotland. It illustrates our conviction.

> The presence of God was a universal, inescapable fact: at home, in the church and by the roadside. The very air seemed to be tingling with divine vitality. One night a man came to a manse in great concern. The minister brought him into the study and asked, "What touched you? I haven't seen you at any of the services." "No," he replied. "I haven't been to church, but this revival is in the air. I can't get away from the Spirit."

In another part the biographer writes,

> In the fields or at the weaving looms, men were overcome and prostrated on the ground before God. One said: "The grass beneath my feet and the rocks around me seem to cry: 'Flee to Christ for refuge!'" The agony of conviction was terrible to behold, but Duncan [Campbell] rejoiced knowing that out of the deep travail would be born a rich, virile Christian experience, unlike the cheap, easy-going "believe-ism" that produces no radical moral change.

That story is the outcome of a great spiritual awakening in which self-sufficient people became thoroughly convicted of sin, repented and were transformed by the love of God.

So what is genuine revival? Revival is the awesome, sustained, manifest presence of God that changes the moral and spiritual life of a community and culture. It is the sovereign outpouring of the Holy Spirit in God's way and time—first of all on God's people. It strongly accentuates the revelation of His holiness and, as a result, His viewpoint on sin. Everyone, young and old, has the opportunity to repent deeply or else harden his or her heart against the convicting power of the Holy Spirit.

Revival is God greatly stirring, shaking and changing His people from apathy, selfishness and self-promotion to desperation, prayer, humility, honesty, contrition and passion for God and His glory and a deep burden for the lost.

Revival is the fullest expression of the life of the Lord Jesus in every believer.

A great spiritual awakening among lost souls also takes place, as multitudes of hardened sinners repent deeply of their sin and commit their lives to the Lord Jesus Christ. Revival is not evangelism, but it inevitably includes a great increase in effective evangelism.

Genuine revival is always related to the Body of Christ.

Spiritual awakening is related to the unconverted.

In revival God does more to extend His Kingdom in seconds and minutes than what takes place in weeks, months or years of usual Christian activity. In genuine revival, the unpredictable and unusual are normal.

During an outpouring of the Holy Spirit among the Zulus in South Africa in the 1970s, many repented openly of sin and experienced great joy in the Lord. Many, but not all.

On one occasion, during a meeting at the church, a fork of lightning—out of a clear, blue sky, without even a sign of rain—suddenly struck the church building on one side, resulting in a large crack on one of the inside walls.

A Christian man in the congregation cried out, "It's me! It's because of me!"

The crack had occurred right beside where he was sitting.

In deep repentance he explained that he had been immoral and had resisted the Holy Spirit's conviction, unwilling to acknowledge his sin until now.

Not long after, a friend of mine visited that church in South Africa and saw the large crack in the wall. He told me that the pastors had purposely left the crack unmended. It was a constant reminder that when we pray for revival, we can expect that everything about God's manifest presence will be accelerated and that it will certainly not be "church as usual."

This account is also a reminder of the truth of Luke 8:17: "For nothing is secret that will not be revealed, nor anything hidden that will not be known and come to light" (if we do not first bring it to the light in repentance, and make restitution where needed).

When we are serious about a real transformation of society, we will pray the following prayers, always starting with humility, until God answers:

"O LORD, though our iniquities testify against us, do it for Your name's sake; for our backslidings are many, we have sinned against You."

Jeremiah 14:7

Gird Your sword upon Your thigh, O Mighty One, with Your glory and Your majesty. And in Your majesty, ride prosperously because of *truth*, *humility*, and *righteousness*; and Your right hand shall teach You awesome things.

Psalm 45:3–4, emphasis added

In genuine revival, we are out of our comfort zones.
It can be very messy.
The display of God's holiness produces deep conviction of sin. Sin is exposed from God's perspective, which is often devastating to experience and listen to—but also wonderfully liberating.

Satanic forces that have been hidden are at times exposed and then overcome by exercising faith in

the name of the Lord Jesus
the written Word of God
the shed blood of the Lord Jesus
the power of the Holy Spirit

The light of God's truth preached in the power of the Holy Spirit exposes the darkness at an accelerated dimension. The invasion of the Holy Spirit's presence and power often pushes human programs aside, giving God's people a whole new perspective on His priorities in relation to having church.

This is what we can expect:

> From the west, men will fear the name of the LORD, and from the rising of the sun, they will revere His glory. For he will come like a pent-up flood that the breath of the LORD drives along.
>
> Isaiah 59:19 NIV1984

A Holy Spirit–energized tsunami.

> For the LORD will rise up as at Mount Perazim, He will be angry as in the Valley of Gibeon—that He may do His work, His awesome work, and bring to pass His act, *His unusual act.*
>
> Isaiah 28:21, emphasis added

> By *awesome deeds* in righteousness You will answer us.
>
> Psalm 65:5, emphasis added

Revival is anything but business as usual. But those who have been crying out to God to show up at any price would not have it any other way.

To my intense delight a close friend of mine, Andy Byrd, has, along with Sean Feucht, coauthored an amazing book titled *Culture of Revival: A Revivalist Field Manual* (Fire and Fragrance, 2012). It is truly one of a kind. Seven other radical lovers of Jesus have made their dynamic contributions to the eleven chapters. This book is not for wimps! It is very intense and helps to describe what I believe I am trying to say right here in this book about genuine revival changing the *culture.*

Only God can start a revival. Man can stop one through resisting, quenching and grieving the Holy Spirit. Only God knows when He's going to respond to the united cries of His people and unleash the Holy Spirit as described in Psalm 45:3–4 (emphasis added):

> Gird Your sword upon Your thigh, O Mighty One, with Your glory and Your majesty. And in Your majesty ride prosperously because of truth, humility and righteousness; and Your right hand shall teach You *awesome things*.

In genuine revival and spiritual awakening, God does more in seconds to extend His Kingdom than in weeks, months or years of our normal God-directed activities. Will you take time to call on God, as a way of life, *until* He breaks through and does what only He can do?

Pray for the Preparation of Spirit-Sent Tsunamis

No man can ever predict how God is going to display His glory and do "awesome things for which we did not look" (or expect). The unusual is the normal. "For when you did awesome things that we did not expect, you came down, and the mountains trembled before you" (Isaiah 64:3 NIV). That is one of the many reasons why we need to regularly pray for spiritual leaders to be prepared for the tsunamis of the Spirit.

I suggest we pray in the following ways:

1. Pray that God will raise up people with a burdened heart for genuine revival, which will be evident by their prayer lives.
2. Pray that God would raise up those who would teach, inspire and encourage others to have a burdened heart for revival from God's Word.
3. Pray that believers will seek God for an understanding of the ways of the Spirit from God's Word and study about how God worked in past revivals.

4. Pray that our existing leaders will be sensitive and flexible, and will flow with whatever new thing God may want to do in any situation, regardless of their traditions and liturgies.

5. Pray that we will be taken over by the fear of the Lord and released from the fear of men. Pray that leaders will recognize that the fear of the Lord is the source of their much-needed wisdom.

6. Pray that we will be given a desire to be radically real and repent of all hypocrisy.

7. Pray that we will be freed from concern for our personal reputations.

8. Pray that influential Christians will be prepared to move beyond their comfort zones and trust God to give them directions when the unusual and unpredictable take place.

9. Pray that if established leaders are unsure what to do, they will have the humility to confer with others—regardless of race or gender—whom they know listen to and obey the Holy Spirit as a way of life.

10. Pray for an openness among God's people, that they will be prepared and ready to be used by God and sent anywhere by Him at any time in revival.

Are we desperate enough to pay the price for the unity Jesus prayed in John 17 that we would have, so that God can answer our prayers for all heaven to break loose in genuine revival and spiritual awakening? The next chapter will give us the blueprint.

2

The Ultimate Model for the Most Fulfilling Relationships

Do you want to experience the most fulfilling, rewarding relationships possible to humankind? Not just with one or two of your closest friends, but with everyone God brings across your path? We know that God, who is love, loves perfectly and unconditionally. But how do we ever begin to function like Him? It seems so unrealistic. So far beyond anything we could think possible. I know, I have been there . . . until one day part of the Godhead, the Holy Spirit, invited me to think of how the most purposeful, practical team ever is able to work together in perfect unity. That thought excited me, and I started thinking about how God the Father, God the Son and God the Holy Spirit function.

But before I could go any further with that thought, the most mind-boggling thought raced alongside that one in my mind, like one runner overtaking another runner on a field track. It went to John 17:22 (kjv), where Jesus is praying to God the Father about *all* His children. Jesus says, "that they may be one, even as we are one."

Wow, what an amazing concept! Could this ever happen to people like you and me?

I thought I had better have a serious look into how this totally successful team of the Trinity functions. What are some of the team members' characteristics? As I pondered, I wrote down the following:

- They are equal in authority, but different in function. That is a basic truth that will affect our understanding of everything else.
- They complete each other in ministry functions—never compete. Often, we are totally unaware of where one starts and another ends. There is a total blending of the three.
- They are absolutely dependent on each other based on their humility, knowing how much they need each other.
- They have absolute truth in their relationships; therefore they have absolute trust.
- They support and serve one another.
- They have singleness of purpose.
- They operate in complete holiness; therefore they experience the ultimate enjoyment of each other.
- The result is an invincible team that has an eternal, indestructible Kingdom; therefore this team is the ultimate in effectiveness.

After these things I heard a loud voice of a great multitude in heaven, saying, "Alleluia! Salvation and glory and honor and power belong to the Lord our God!"

Revelation 19:1

34

And I heard, as it were, the voice of a great multitude, as the sound of many waters and as the sound of mighty thunderings, saying, "Alleluia! For the Lord God Omnipotent reigns!"

Revelation 19:6

Now I saw heaven opened, and behold, a white horse. And He who sat on him was called Faithful and True, and in righteousness He judges and makes war. His eyes were like a flame of fire, and on His head were many crowns. He had a name written that no one knew except Himself. He was clothed with a robe dipped in blood, and His name is called The Word of God.

Revelation 19:11–13

And He has on His robe and on His thigh a name written: KING OF KINGS AND LORD OF LORDS.

Revelation 19:16

Wow again, what a quintessential team for success. Can we operate with those characteristics in all our relationships? If we believe that God the Father always answers Jesus' prayers, we can. And if we believe that as we daily surrender our lives to Jesus and ask for the Holy Spirit's control, believing that He takes over . . . then He will enable us to live by the same characteristics.

Unbelief will block and stop God's power in and through us. Treat it as you would a plague. Don't go there. "Without faith it is impossible to please God" (Hebrews 11:6 NIV).

This wonderful, workable, biblical Trinity unity is what God intends us to experience here on earth, and it hurts His heart if we are not doing so.

Okay, so someone may think, *If you only knew what I've been through, you'd understand that I can't trust anyone anymore. So that rules out the whole deal for me. And how could I ever expect the Trinity God to even understand my pain?*

I understand that reaction, I really do! But let me explain something about this utterly amazing triune God. He not only knows all about your pain, but knows how you feel. He has been there!

And because of that, God's Word tells us in Hebrews 7:25 that Jesus is always praying to the Father on behalf of His children's needs, and nothing is beyond His control. Better still, Psalm 147:5 says, "His understanding is infinite." That is total understanding of the cause and extent of what we have suffered.

Let's go back to Jesus' prayer to His Father God in John 17:20–21, "I do not pray for these alone, but also for those who will believe in Me through their word; that they all may be one . . . that the world may believe that You sent Me." Again in verse 23, Jesus prays, "I in them, and You in Me; that they may be made perfect in one, and that the world may know that You have sent Me, and have loved them as You have loved Me." From these verses we understand that this Trinity unity is a powerfully convincing proof to everyone of the following two things:

- That God the Father sent God the Son to earth in the person of the Lord Jesus Christ.
- That God the Father loves His disciples on earth today equally as He loves His Son.

The Power and Force of Unity

Here is another way of understanding the importance and weight of these truths. Trinity unity operating in God's children, the Body of Christ, will be the *primary incentive* for the world to recognize these two things:

1. The deity of the Lord Jesus.
2. The total commitment of the Godhead to every disciple of the Lord Jesus.

So, Jesus did not say it would take more prayer and fasting, or more preaching, or more witnessing or more power evangelism, as important as they all are, to convince the world of those two things. It would take one thing above them all—*Trinity unity*.

The power and force of this unity cannot be hidden. It is glowingly obvious to non-Christians. And according to John 17:22 (ESV), the source of it is the same glory that God the Father gave to His Son, and it shines through His disciples. "The glory that you have given me I have given to them, that they may be one even as we are one."

This in turn strongly motivates non-Christians to commit their lives to the Lord Jesus Christ.

Matthew 12:25 (ESV) says "Every kingdom divided against itself is laid waste, and no city or house divided against itself will stand." We are only as strong and effective as we are united.

We must conclude that the greatest key to reaching more souls so they will come into Christ's Kingdom is in His disciples' operating in Trinity unity. Quite a conclusion! That really must be the greatest reason why God has spoken to me so clearly to write this book.

United we stand. Divided we fall.

Trinity Dynamics

Now let's take a closer look into the relational dynamics within the Trinity. Before God created man and gave him a free will, the Godhead agreed upon a plan. If the creature disobeyed the Creator, then the Lord Jesus would pay the full price of God's righteous judgment against sin. He would come down to the earth as a baby and live just like us. Then He would be despised and rejected by the creatures He created and finally crucified on a Roman cross. By so doing, He would pay the full penalty for every sin ever committed—the worst of all of it—for the worst and the best of us. Romans 3:23 says, "For all have sinned and fall short of the glory of God."

I cannot begin to imagine the intense agony of the Father God at seeing His beloved Son being scourged as the Roman soldiers lacerated His back with 39 stripes from a whip with spikes in it. Then, with a crown of thorns riveted to His head, they ordered Him to carry His cross to the place of public crucifixion. Jesus retained His nature of deity as Son of God while operating solely in our humanity as Son of Man when on the earth. That is why His suffering mentally, spiritually and physically was so intense. No one has ever suffered such agony—and has been so totally innocent.

Could it be that one of the reasons why the sun was completely darkened for the three hours that Jesus was on the cross . . . when Jesus cried out to His Father, "My God, my God, why have you forsaken me?" . . . was that the Father's agony in having to put all the punishment for the sins of the world upon His beloved Son was so great that He could not bear to expose the scene to the light of day any longer?

Second Corinthians 5:21 tells us that "He [God] made Him [Jesus] who knew no sin to be sin for us." That means all the accumulated filth of the sins of the world was somehow heaped upon Him. That this display of unconditional love and incomprehensible humility has been recorded in God's holy Word leaves me in absolute awe and wonder and deep gratitude. And I can choose to receive Jesus' free gift of salvation or reject it.

Then I ponder the role of the Holy Spirit during the crucifixion. I believe He was agonizing over the suffering of God the Father, as well as over Jesus the Son. How could it be otherwise, because of the unclouded communion the Trinity had always experienced? Oh, the unspeakable agony of the Trinity!

All this, that you and I may be assured of our sins being forgiven and of having eternal life in unclouded relationship with our wonderful Creator. Our part is to acknowledge that we are sinners, turn away from our sins, thank Jesus for dying for us and ask Him to come into our hearts, by faith receiving Him as our Savior and making Him Lord of our life.

Now, back to the Trinity. Try to imagine the exquisite joy in heaven when Jesus returned to be enthroned at His Father's right hand—knowing that the Holy Spirit had gone down to earth to indwell and empower all of Jesus' disciples who would yield to Him and obey Him. What an almighty celebration reunion that would have been!

I love the beautiful encouragements God has for us in the next chapter.

3

The Uniqueness of Trinity Unity

According to Psalm 133:3, the results of living this biblical Trinity unity are inevitable. God uses a strong word when He says He *commands* the blessing—life forevermore. It is as though God is saying that whatever else you do not have prioritized in your group situation, if you will make sure you are united in vision, all called of God, operating in your ministry giftings and have the right attitude of heart toward God and others, then He will make sure He shows up in a way we will all know.

Wow, I will go for that! Let's look at Psalm 133:1–3 (NIV):

> How good and pleasant it is when God's people live together in unity! It is like precious oil poured on the head, running down on the beard, running down on Aaron's beard, down on the collar of his robe. It is as if the dew of Hermon were falling on Mount Zion. For there the LORD bestows his blessing, even life forevermore.

The following story vividly illustrates these truths. Soon after the Los Angeles riots in 1992, Dr. Lloyd Ogilvie, then pastor of

First Presbyterian Church of Hollywood, and Dr. Ken Ulmer, pastor of then-named Faithful Central Missionary Baptist Church (from the riot-devastated area of Los Angeles), along with some members of their congregations, joined with Pastor Jack Hayford and many of us at The Church On The Way in Van Nuys, California, for a Sunday night service. The manifest presence of the living Christ was absolutely awesome. Unfortunately, the word *awesome* is often used to describe ice cream or a person or whatever, whereas it should only be used to describe the only One who is truly awesome—God Himself!

And this night God's presence was truly *awesome*. The atmosphere was thick with God! I believe this was a direct result of the deeper levels of humility, love and commitment to one another that were openly expressed by these three spiritual leaders who had been close friends for years.

On the platform the three pastors quietly and reverently served each other in communion, and then made serious commitments to each other before God and man. The large multiracial, joint congregation was then instructed to find someone of a different race, and with whom we had not previously prayed, and partner with them in serving each other communion. What a uniquely powerful time that was. Inevitably, the three congregations that were represented experienced new levels of unity with each other.

The sense of God's approving presence was so tangibly strong that I seriously wondered how that service could ever be closed. We started at 5:00 that evening and finished after 9:00 p.m. The next day when I was in conversation with a senior member of the pastoral staff, we agreed that we could not remember a stronger sense of God's awesome presence in the history of this church. God was demonstrating His approval of this display of the unity for which Jesus prayed in John 17, and the blessing God promised in Psalm 133 came.

In Psalm 133, biblical unity is likened to the oil that ran down over the head, beard and collar of Aaron the priest's garment. The description of that oil is found in Exodus 30:22–32. The oil is very costly, very holy and very fragrant. Let's look at how that applies to us today.

This Oil Is Very Costly

Bible unity is not peace at any price. It requires our "speaking the truth in love," which means dealing with situations that are at times difficult and can be painful. We must humble ourselves when needed, and, just as importantly, release forgiveness and unconditional love to others.

During the time I was writing this manuscript, my husband, Jim, and I needed to meet with a spiritual leader whom we dearly love and respect. I was very aware that the items on our agenda could well be challenged, possibly strongly. Before our meeting, I was doing my daily reading of the Bible and 1 Timothy 1:5 was strongly quickened to me: "Now the purpose of the commandment is love from a pure heart, from a good conscience, and from sincere faith."

I realized that everything we were about to share had to pass those requirements to have God's favor. "A pure heart" means the motives have to be solely for the glory of God. "A good conscience" means that we have no known, undealt-with sin in our lives, before God and men. "From sincere faith" means that we must be releasing genuine faith that God will work among us to reveal His will and purposes.

When I shared this with Jim and our leader friend, they both agreed with the truths and implications. We handed over our agenda and time together into the hands of the Holy Spirit and believed He was in control.

In that meeting, strong exchanges of convictions took place. New information needed sharing. Presumptions needed correcting. Strong affirmations were declared. And when deep convictions obviously differed, we all expressed humility by declaring that we would seek God diligently until His mind was clearly revealed to both parties. We again affirmed our genuine love for each other.

I believe what could easily have been a tense time of painful disagreements actually eventuated into a deeper bonding of the love and unity I am writing about. "Thank You, Lord."

This Oil Is Very Holy

Exodus 30:25 says, "And you shall make from these a holy anointing oil, an ointment compounded according to the art of the perfumer. It shall be a holy anointing oil."

God wants us to understand that the Bible's standards of holiness in all our relationships are far removed from what is so often accepted and/or tolerated by many—including so-called mature Christian leaders.

The Bible says, "As he thinks in his heart, so is he" (Proverbs 23:7). Would we want our thought lives to be written out so all could see? I believe Jesus could have been doing some of that when He wrote with His finger on the ground, as the Pharisees stood around condemning the woman caught in adultery (see John 8:8).

Would every preacher want his or her thought life while preaching written on a wall behind him or her by the finger of God? God's finger sovereignly appeared on King Belshazzar's banquet wall, pronouncing his doom (see Daniel 5:24–28). God can do that again anytime. How? Because He is God, awesome in holiness, pristine in purity and limitless in power. "Mountains melt like wax before the LORD" (Psalm 97:5 NIV).

God's standard of holiness means our living within the biblical standards of holiness in thought, word and actions, and our repenting of all that does not meet those standards.

This Oil Is Very Fragrant

Being fragrant means this oil is delicate, beautiful and pleasurable.

We are unable to enjoy each other as God intended where there is undealt-with sin in any relationship. Satan tempts us by trying to convince us otherwise. He says, "Add just a little bit of sin to it, and it will become more exciting." If we fall for that one, he says, "Add a lot more sin to it, and it will be more fulfilling."

The more we listen to those lies, the farther away we become from experiencing the wonders of Trinity unity, which is also described in Psalm 133 as the dew which falls on Mount Hermon in Israel. Dew is absolutely essential for life on that mountain since little rain falls on it.

I believe God is saying that the quality of our spiritual lives, related to extending the Kingdom of God on the earth, is determined by the quality of our unity with all the other members of Christ's Body. And we will outsmart the devil every time when we fulfill these conditions of Trinity unity. Satan is full of pride; therefore he has no wisdom. "When pride comes, then comes disgrace, but with the humble is wisdom" (Proverbs 11:2 ESV).

Do we sense the need for a fresh anointing of the Holy Spirit on our lives and ministries? As we humble ourselves before God at the deepest levels of adoration, worship and praise to Him for who He is, the Holy Spirit will at times manifest the literal fragrance of Jesus' person and presence.

For over three decades, I had the privilege and pleasure of having Mary Lance Sisk as one of my dearest and most trusted friends. In April 2012, she went to heaven unexpectedly in her sleep, to be with her precious Lord and Master. One of my most treasured memories of her is when she shared the following incident during the last of our numerous phone conversations.

Mary Lance was invited to speak at a women's conference meeting in a large hotel in a city in the U.S. She was scheduled to speak at the first session in the morning and had risen at 5:00 a.m. to spend quality time in the Word of God and in prayer. She said she had spent a protracted time pouring out her heart in devotion to the Lord, lying face down on her hotel room floor. Later, when she got into the hotel elevator on her way to the conference room, there were two other women with her who obviously were not conferees. Both of them remarked on the exquisite perfume in the air and immediately wanted to know the brand name of the one Mary Lance had used that morning.

My precious friend quietly but firmly assured them that she did not use perfume and that this morning was no exception— not that she was averse to those who do. Their response was unbelief, as neither of them had used any perfume that day.

The Holy Spirit gave my friend, this radical Jesus lover, the understanding that those women were sensing the fragrance that emanated from her being close to "the rose of Sharon" so long in worship during those early morning hours. "He who is joined to the Lord is one spirit with Him" (1 Corinthians 6:17). And 2 Corinthians 2:15 explains, as perhaps no other passage, the fragrance that emanates from our lives when we live these biblical principles: "For we are to God the fragrance of Christ among those who are being saved and among those who are perishing."

In the next chapter, we will find out how this unity works in practice for you and me.

4

How This Unity Works

We must believe it is possible for this biblical unity to become a reality. Before Lazarus was raised from the dead, Jesus said to those standing around, "Take away the stone" (see John 11:39). Many times the "stone" is our unbelief and hardness of heart about simply believing God's Word before we experience His supernatural power operating in our lives. If we do believe, we are ready for the next step.

We must want to experience unity with all the rest of God's children—regardless of their ethnicity, denominational affiliation, educational status or lack of it, how young or old they are, how long they have put their faith in Christ; rich or poor, smart or dull of understanding. Period.

When the apostle Paul was giving the Colossian Christians the reason why he was thankful to God for them, he wrote, "Since we heard of your faith in Christ Jesus and of your love for *all* the saints" (Colossians 1:4, emphasis added).

Okay, let's think about who some of "*all* the saints" might be. How about the Pygmies in Africa who are still following tribal ways of living? Or the traditional hunter-gatherer Aboriginals in the remotest parts of Australia? Can we easily say and mean that we could esteem them as greater than ourselves?

I have thought about how the Christians among them must be strong in faith. They probably have to believe for God's help to get most every meal. They would have to find enough game to survive. They would have to be very adept with their weapons to hunt down enough wild animals to make a meal for all. Their prayers for God's help would be simple and direct. And their survival would depend on their faith to believe that God saw their need and was interested enough and able to supply on a daily basis.

The truth is, they could probably teach us a whole lot about the rest of faith Paul talks about in Hebrews 3 and 4, and the God of the miraculous supply. How God would love hearing their prayers after they wake up in the morning. Perhaps such a prayer goes something like this:

> My heavenly Dad, You've done it again—turned on a beautiful day! I will be joyful and give You thanks. I'm so glad You're interested in my practical needs because I really would love to have eggs for breakfast. You and I know birds' eggs are hard to find, and they're so far up in the trees, but I'm asking You to lead me to the right tree and help me to get them—without breaking them. Your Book says if I ask anything in Jesus' name, believing, You will answer. So here goes. This is exactly my request. And I'm excited to see You do what You say You will.

Off the praying hunter runs. Later, he comes back to camp with a grin from ear to ear and halfway down his back! Over his fire, he thanks his heavenly Dad for meeting his needs *again*—for the umpteenth time!

Paul was grateful to God and enthusiastic about the Thessalonian believers when he wrote them, "We are bound to thank

God always for you, brethren, as it is fitting, because your faith grows exceedingly, and the love of every one of you all abounds toward each other" (2 Thessalonians 1:3).

Did you notice that in these quotations Paul links faith and love together—with faith first? When we believe that God wants this Trinity unity for you and me, then we can trust Him to give us His love for everyone. It is an unconditional love.

That is God's part.

Our part is to ask for it. "You do not have because you do not ask" (James 4:2). And we must receive it by faith. "Whatever is not from faith is sin" (Romans 14:23).

Before we go any further, we need to be thoroughly convinced that this kind of love is entirely supernatural. The greatest saints who have ever lived have never been able to experience it, outside of the Holy Spirit doing a supernatural, miraculous work in their hearts to produce it.

The following story illustrates this truth. It is taken from Mr. Jim Green's letters related to the showing of the *JESUS* film on November 29, 2011. (Jim Green is the former executive director of The *JESUS* Film Project, which is an outreach of Campus Crusade for Christ International.)

A "JESUS" film team was courageously taking the film into a "hard-core" anti-Christian area, right in the midst of a religious festival where thousands had gathered.

When radicals realized that the team was Christian, and had come with news of a "foreign religion," they became enraged. They stirred up an angry mob of 300 people, surrounding and rocking the vehicle, striking the windows with sticks and rocks. Breaking through the glass, they dragged the team leader, Marwan, to the ground, beating him ferociously.

The mob also grabbed all the film equipment—the screen, generator, projector, and four reels of "JESUS," and placed it in a pile. They doused the equipment with gasoline and set it ablaze. Smoke billowed skyward as Marwan took blow after blow. Blood began pouring from his eyes. A policeman saw the commotion and tried to intervene, but he could not break through the crowd. The mob attempted to throw Marwan into the fire and burn him to death. But then something wondrous happened.

Instantly, Marwan was not alone. Though the blows kept coming, and the crowd raged around him, Marwan sensed something very powerful . . . more like Someone. Marwan said it was like the arms of protection had wrapped around him, shielding him from the worst of the attack, and keeping him from the flames. At last, one policeman penetrated through the crowd and pulled Marwan to safety.

Sadly, all the equipment was destroyed and Marwan spent days in the hospital. But he survived, as well as his team. Then Marwan did something amazing. Six months later he went back to his attackers ". . . *to preach the Good News where the name of Christ has never been heard.*"

The people immediately recognized Marwan . . . and were incredulous. They had tried to kill him, but now he had come back, was joyous, without fear of death. The people told Marwan how the ring leaders of his savage attack had died a few weeks earlier, killed in a motorcycle crash. He again offered to show them the film, "JESUS." Because of his courage, they said they would watch.

Marwan's team showed "JESUS" several times . . . without resistance. The people met the Lord for the first time; were moved by His words, His love, miracles, death, and resurrection . . . things they had never known before. Many were stunned. The Holy Spirit affirmed as truth all they were seeing and hearing in their mother tongue. Hundreds responded.

And I wish you could meet Marwan today. He would tell you with joy and satisfaction that there is now a thriving church in that very community. So much has happened since the attack and his Divine protection. He would also tell you that because of people's giving and prayers, he and the teams he leads are showing "JESUS" ever deeper into the most resistant of places. He would speak of tens of thousands who, upon hearing the gospel for the first time, are saying "yes" to Jesus. May His name be praised!

How do we get there? We submit to the person of the Holy Spirit, who alone can work it in us and through us. "The love of God has been poured out in our hearts by the Holy Spirit who was given to us" (Romans 5:5).

I love the following quote from Dr. A. B. Simpson's *When the Comforter Came* (Christian Publications, 1991):

> The Holy Spirit kindles in the soul the fires of love . . . the flame that melts our selfishness and pours out our being in tenderness, sacrifice, and service. And the same fire of love is the fusing, uniting flame which makes Christians one; just as the volcanic tide that rolls down the mountain fuses into one current everything in its course.

We now come to another major condition in order for this miracle love to function. Simply put, we must realize that humility of heart is the only condition that this Trinity love will work in. Humility is the basis of all genuine love. All lack of love is based in pride. All coldness of heart is rooted in pride. We are only as loving as we are truly humble. God's Word makes this clear:

> So if there is any encouragement in Christ, any incentive of love, any participation in the Spirit, any affection and sympathy, complete my joy by being of the same mind, having the same love, being in full accord and of one mind. *Do nothing from selfishness or conceit, but in humility count others better than yourselves.* Let each of you look not only to his own interests, but also to the interests of others.
>
> Philippians 2:1–4 RSV, emphasis added

The key is verse 3. The heavier our responsibilities are, the less likely we will see the need to be attentive to the needs of others. Again, humility is the key.

I have always been impressed with how Jesus demonstrated this in a very practical way. Early in the morning, He went to the trouble of getting fresh fish and pita bread, gathered enough firewood and kindling to make a decent campfire on the beach, and cooked and served a great breakfast for His young disciples. I have often wondered where He got the pan, plates and utensils at such an early hour—and He would not forget the salt and a bag for scraps. What a humble servant leader!

We are only as united as we are loving.

We are only as loving as we are humble.

Paul the apostle, writing from prison, says, "I . . . beg you to lead a life worthy of the calling to which you have been called, with all lowliness and meekness, with patience, forbearing one another in love, eager to maintain the unity of the Spirit in the bond of peace" (Ephesians 4:1–3 RSV).

The Divine order is:

Humility

Love

Unity

Peace

In the next chapter, we are going a little deeper into the how-tos, so stay with me for the ride.

5

Principles Needed for Unity
to Work in Any Group

It is important to understand that four principles in the ways
of God must be at work in order for Trinity unity to work
in any group—whether the group is made up of two people or
two thousand. Let's take a look at those four vital principles.

First, *we must be called of God to that particular group.*
Here are two examples. John 1:6 says, "There was a man sent
from God, whose name was John." John 3:34 (RSV) says, "For
He whom God has sent utters the words of God."

We must guard against presumption by making sure that we
have heard from God before joining any group of God's people.
"Keep back Your servant also from presumptuous sins; let them
not have dominion over me. Then I shall be blameless, and I
shall be innocent of great transgression" (Psalm 19:13).

If we do not obey these biblical injunctions, we will always
feel like a square peg in a round hole, no matter how spiritual

we or the others in the group are. And in time, we will become aware of disunity.

We have a wonderful promise in Psalm 32:8: "I will instruct you and teach you in the way you should go; I will guide you with My eye." As we seek God earnestly in faith, He will make known to us what we are to do.

Second, *we must all have the same vision and purpose.* "Where there is no vision, the people cast off restraint" (Proverbs 29:18 ESV).

It is the responsibility of the spiritual leaders to seek God's face for His vision for the group they have been called to lead. Vision is not program. Program fits vision. The vision is the most far-reaching purpose in God's heart, for which He brings a group into existence.

Leaders should also frequently ask God, "Is there more vision You want to give me?" The vision should be clearly defined and declared to the people. The leadership is then responsible to implement the vision and is accountable to God.

Third, *this unity can only be achieved as all members of a group are functioning in their respective ministry gifts*, as outlined in Romans 12:6–8, 1 Corinthians 12:28 and Ephesians 4:11–12.

In addition, Ephesians 4:11–12 makes it clear that it is only as we have the fivefold ministry giftings operating in the Body of Christ that we can expect to have the full Trinity unity Jesus intends for all His children: "And He Himself gave some to be apostles, some prophets, some evangelists, and some pastors and teachers, for the equipping of the saints for the work of ministry, for the edifying of the body of Christ."

There are other ministry gifts, such as the ministry of helps, hospitality, writing, giving, many forms of worship and music and numbers of others. It is so important to know what our individual ministry giftings are so that we are not functioning outside of our boundaries and causing disunity.

It is equally important to know what other people's ministries in our group are so that the leaders can release them to function in those giftings. All can then learn and receive from them and be blessed. Galatians 5:13 says, "Through love serve one another," and Ephesians 5:21 says, "Submitting to one another in the fear of God."

I will share more about the ministries in the next chapter. Paul must have had in mind some believers who were starting out in their ministry giftings when he wisely exhorted us all in Romans 12:16 (RSV), "Live in harmony with one another; do not be haughty, but associate with the lowly; never be conceited."

Again, humility is the key to the love and unity.

Fourth, *we must always have the right attitude of heart toward God and others in the group.*

You may think, *Why question our attitude toward God?* The more responsibility we have, the more likely we are to carry resentment (maybe hidden) toward God related to serving Him—because of the weight of our responsibilities. Leaders need to frequently ask the Holy Spirit if they have any hidden resentment toward God related to serving Him.

Campbell McAlpine, a British Bible teacher of depth and a very Christlike man of God, was a dear friend of mine for many years. We were often teamed together to speak at spiritual leadership conferences in different nations. The price was high and we were often exhausted, yet with never a complaint, Campbell would say as a way of life, "It's such a privilege and pleasure to serve You, Lord." It helped remind me of my own teaching, "The privilege is always higher than the price."

To maintain God's standard of unity, we also must have no reserves in our hearts toward others. A reserve unchecked will produce coldness, aloofness, resentment, judging, criticism, lack of confidence, lack of fellowship, lack of love and lack of unity. Holding on to a reserve is doing less than what 1 Peter 1:22

describes: "Love one another fervently with a pure heart." The Greek word there for *fervently* means "boiling point."

The Reverend Neville Horne was one of the most Christlike people I have ever met. He was a Baptist minister from Sydney, Australia, who stayed with us in our home for ten days when we lived in New Zealand. One day, he quietly shared with me in passing that every hour, he stopped to check in with the Holy Spirit to see if he had grieved Him in any way. That impacted me deeply.

James 3:1 (ESV) says, "We who teach shall be judged with greater strictness." Why? Because greater knowledge brings greater accountability. And God does not want to multiply phonies!

Now let's face the facts—obviously, most evangelical Christians who sincerely want many more lost souls to come to the saving knowledge of the Lord Jesus Christ cannot be taking this subject of biblical unity seriously. Why do I say that? Because we pour infinitely more effort and money into reaching the lost than we do into fulfilling biblical standards of unity. We spend more time preaching the Gospel in churches and on TV, on the radio and on the Internet, distributing tracts, having prayer conferences and prayer meetings, and doing personal evangelism and mass evangelistic crusades than we spend humbling ourselves before God and each other and living God's standards of unconditional love for one another.

Second Chronicles 7:14 is one of the most misquoted Scriptures related to getting God's attention to heal a nation. It does not *first* say, "If My people who are called by My Name will *pray*." God *first* says, "If they will *humble* themselves . . ." It is one thing to get God's people together to pray; it is quite another thing to get them to acknowledge and repent of the pride that causes divisions—ethnically, generationally, gender-wise, denominationally, maritally, in interfamily relationships, and between leaders and staff, teachers and students, employers and employees, and siblings.

Pride is our greatest sin.

How do I know? When Lucifer first tempted Eve and Adam in the Garden of Eden, he tried to get them to doubt God's instructions. That would be the sin of unbelief. But the sin of pride is always the basis of unbelief. True humility does not question the authority and authenticity of the only One who has made the world by His spoken words and upholds the universe by the word of His power. "Who being the brightness of His glory and the express image of His person, and upholding all things by the word of His power, when He had by Himself purged our sins, sat down at the right hand of the Majesty on high" (Hebrews 1:3). The root of all sins is first pride, then unbelief.

The Bible has a special word of caution and warning to husbands and wives. The apostle Peter, who was married, says in essence that married couples' prayers can be hindered if they are not operating in a sensitive, loving relationship with each other. "Husbands, likewise, dwell with them with understanding, giving honor to the wife, as to the weaker vessel, and as being heirs together of the grace of life, *that your prayers may not be hindered*" (1 Peter 3:7, emphasis added).

It is possible to be the head of the largest or most effective prayer movement that we know of and not be living in a humble, loving, devoted, servant role with our wives or husbands (there are many women prayer leaders). Disunity hinders our effectiveness in our prayer ministries. And God is unimpressed with all our efforts. What a tragic waste of time and energy.

The next chapter was by far the most challenging for me to write. By not compromising any biblical truths, I realize that I may have rocked the boat of centuries of traditions.

6

The Importance of the Ministries and Unity

There is an enormous breakdown of unity in the Body of Christ because the ministries are not functioning together as God intended. The remedy starts with an understanding of the ministries themselves and how they complement each other. I want to share some basic truths on this subject. This is certainly not intended as a comprehensive biblical presentation of this big subject, but I have gleaned these truths over many years of studying God's Word.

God has a divine order in which the ministries function. It is all in the blueprint of His Word for those who want to follow it, regardless of how the denominations, missionary organizations, churches or groups have chosen to operate. First, let's look at the order the ministries come in:

And God has appointed these in the church: first apostles, second prophets, third teachers, after that miracles, then gifts of healings, helps, administrations, varieties of tongues.

1 Corinthians 12:28

And He Himself gave some to be apostles, some prophets, some evangelists, and some pastors and teachers.

Ephesians 4:11

Just so we do not miss the importance of God's order, we see it again in Ephesians 2:20 (KJV), which says the household of God is "built upon the foundation of the apostles and prophets." That leads me to a simple illustration. The ministries appear as the basic structural functions for a house:

The apostles represent the concrete.

The prophets represent the steel.

(*These are the foundations. We cannot have one without the other.*)

The evangelist represents the doors.

The teacher represents the framework and the dividing walls.

The pastor/teacher represents the roof and windows—the shepherd/covering.

The apostles, prophets, evangelists and pastors often have a teaching ministry in addition. Those with an apostolic ministry usually have some measure of each of the other ministry gifts operating through them, because they are the pioneering foundational ministry and often have to start a work on their own initially. The temptation, then, is for them to think they do not need to function with a prophetic ministry. But Ephesians 2:20 is clear and plain. They do. Concrete without steel will not work for a foundation!

It is all the more important, therefore, that those with an apostolic ministry recognize in humility their need to function close to the prophetic ministries, initially and ongoing. As a prophet/teacher, Silas teamed closely in ministry with both Paul and Barnabas as apostles/teachers.

As God brings people across their paths, all of the fivefold ministries should be seeking God's direction about whom they should release into their individual ministry giftings. This brings great unity and fulfillment to all concerned.

In the early Church, believers had no titles, just ministry functions that they recognized, respected and were led by. The apostles appointed elders, who were the overseers of a local church. The literal meaning of the word *bishop* is "overseer," according to the New King James Version. In Titus 1:5, Paul writes to Titus that he should set in order the things that are lacking by appointing elders in every city, as Paul had instructed him.

The apostles, prophets and elders were the spiritual covering for the Church, giving general oversight. They were only effective to the degree that they were in Trinity unity, waiting on God and receiving directions from the Holy Spirit. A significant understanding came to the early Church in Acts 6, when the spiritual eldership realized that to fulfill their ministries, they needed to continually prioritize their time by giving themselves "to prayer and to the ministry of the word" (verse 5).

That mandate has never changed. Oh what greater depth of teaching, what expanded vision and burden to reach the lost, what changes in conforming more to the image of Christ, what deeper and broader levels of unity would come to the Body of Christ universally if the apostles and prophets would discipline themselves to fulfill this mandate of the Holy Spirit!

Taking a step of obedience toward devoting themselves to prayer and the Word, the early leaders appointed deacons in the Church, who then took care of the many necessary administrative duties.

I love how the Bible makes it very clear that strength of character is a priority with God when spiritual leadership roles are mentioned. When Paul writes to Timothy, he outlines the qualifications for all overseers. We need to heed these qualifications, given in 1 Timothy 3:2–7, and take them seriously at all times. Also, the biblical qualifications for deacons and their wives are outlined directly after that, in verses 8–12. Are we familiar with all these qualifications? Are we living by these standards? It is significant to notice in verses 14–15 (NIV) that Paul thought it was important to reiterate to these two distinctly different ministry functions his purpose in outlining their characteristics:

> Although I hope to come to you soon, I am writing you these instructions so that, if I am delayed, you will know how people ought to conduct themselves in God's household, which is the church of the living God, the pillar and foundation of the truth.

Acts 14:23 records that after much evangelism in Iconium, Lystra, Derbe and Antioch, the apostles Paul and Barnabas "had appointed elders in every church, and prayed with fasting," and then they "commended them to the Lord."

In 1 Timothy 5:17 Paul honors spiritual overseers—apostles, prophets and appointed elders—when he writes, "Let the elders who rule well be counted worthy of double honor, especially those who labor in the word and doctrine." And Hebrews 11:2 shows us how important strong faith is in order for them to fully function in those ministries: "For by it [faith] the elders obtained a good testimony."

No one ministry dominated over another in the early Church, because they really believed in the priesthood of all believers. There was no such thing as clergy and laity, and pastors were certainly not the dominant speakers. I have read that statistically, on a yearly basis, a higher percentage of pastors resign than the percentage of people who resign from other professions. I also have read that every year, approximately three thousand churches in America close down. The following questions arise:

- Did the pastors who quit ever have a genuine direction from the Lord to be pastors/teachers?
- Did they have a call from the Lord to be in full-time Christian ministry but perhaps not know what else to apply for, other than to pastor a church?
- Was it confirmed, either by an apostolic or prophetic ministry or by a mature, seasoned elder, that these people were pastors/teachers?
- Did God confirm from His Word or in some other valid way that the timing was right for these people to take on pastoral responsibilities?

If people have had clear direction from the Lord to be in a ministry position, then they need an equally clear direction from the Lord to leave. And their leaving should be confirmed by the ministries to whom they are submitted.

The Word of God says, "The fear of the LORD is the beginning of knowledge" and "The fear of the LORD is the beginning of wisdom" (Proverbs 1:7; 9:10). Fearing the Lord also means "to hate evil" (Proverbs 8:13), and it is the only thing that releases us from the fear of man. "The fear of man brings a snare" (Proverbs 29:25). The fear of the Lord is therefore essential to maintaining any ministry function with authority.

I have seen far too many godly, dedicated, gifted leaders in ministry who have been frustrated and confused because they did not understand what their ministry functions were, as outlined in God's Word. This resulted in serious problems when people would ask them to fulfill some ministry need and expect them to do it. These leaders would take on those responsibilities, only to find they were often on overload, which inevitably led to a lack of peace and joy . . . and then disunity in their closest relationships.

In some instances, it only took teaching such as I am writing here to reveal to them what their true ministry callings were. Then they would see the need to keep within the boundaries of these ministry functions.

Recently I was with a pastor/teacher, two prophet/teachers and an apostle/teacher—all of whom had truly humble, loving, servant-oriented hearts. Trinity love was flowing like a river, and they wanted truth at any price. Regardless of the fact that they all had great scope and influence in their ministries, they all shared that they greatly needed to have a fresh and new understanding of what the Bible says about the ministries and how they function.

We talked about these things, and as a result, in essence, this is what came in my mail the next week, in a note from two of them: "Thank you for our night of destiny and how the Holy Spirit used the biblical truths you shared to help us put our lives and ministries in order for a movement. Words cannot properly express the gratefulness in our hearts."

Their humility and gratitude impacted and greatly encouraged me, especially in relation to writing this chapter.

Someone may say, "That all sounds great. But where do I start? How do I get a ministry?"

The simple answer is, by obeying the next little thing God tells you to do—and making that a way of life. That is not complicated.

You may ask, "Do I need to announce to others what my ministry is?"

The answer is no. When God sees it is the right time for our ministries to function, He will direct others to be aware of it and release us into them.

"God Will Always Make a Way for Those Who Believe and Obey" is the title of a message I first gave in Seoul, South Korea, to a large gathering of university students and YWAMers in the early seventies. The effects of that message are still reverberating around the earth. I recently met a mature, godly missionary/ teacher who had heard that message as a young woman. She let me know beyond any doubt how it had become a "life message" to her during her many missionary journeys.

Nobody can stop or hinder God's purposes for our lives— other than we ourselves. "I know that You can do everything, and that no purpose of Yours can be withheld from You" (Job 42:2). The devil cannot stop God's purposes. He can only try by tempting us to the age-old methods of pride and/or unbelief that he presented to Adam and Eve in Genesis 3:1–5.

I vividly remember when God first opened up the doors for me to teach the Word of God in seven nations of the world. Jim and I never had a penny to put toward purchasing the necessary round-the-world airplane ticket, nor any knowledge of where the funds would come from. We never shared that need with anyone else, and no one who had invited me took any responsibility for helping me with any of my expenses. We lived in New Zealand at that time.

Suddenly at 2:30 a.m., I was awakened with a voice I immediately recognized as satanic. It was saying to me, "No one will ever give you anything toward that airline ticket you need."

Instantly, the precious Holy Spirit reminded me of Acts 27:25 (RSV), where Paul, aboard a ship about to be wrecked in a great storm, said, "I have faith in God that it will be exactly as I have been told [by the Lord]." I spoke it with authority and resisted the enemy in Jesus' name, and went straight back to sleep. All the money I needed came in slowly but surely from the most unusual sources, without our saying a word to anyone. Hallelujah.

Psalm 138:8 (ESV) says, "The LORD will fulfill his purpose for me." And I love quoting Job 23:13–14 (RSV), "But he is unchangeable and who can turn him? What he desires, that he does. For he will complete what he appoints for me; and many such things are in his mind."

Jim and I watched God fulfill those promises repeatedly as we sought to put God's interests first and to make sure we were living in Trinity unity, which is His standard of righteousness. "But seek first the kingdom of God and His righteousness, and all these things shall be added to you" (Matthew 6:33).

By God's grace, I have never taught the Word of God on any occasion without being in complete unity with my husband. He was my most committed personal intercessor . . . what an incredible gift. How I miss him! But if we were not in unity according to 1 Peter 3:7, those prayers would have been relatively ineffective: "Husbands, likewise, dwell with them with understanding, giving honor to the wife, as to the weaker vessel, and as being heirs together of the grace of life, *that your prayers may not be hindered*" (emphasis added). A sobering thought.

Lack of unity in the Body of Christ holds back the coming of the King. Another sobering thought.

What will it take for God's people to take seriously this subject of Trinity unity? I am praying that this book will help enlighten the Church to see it from God's perspective and make the needed lifestyle changes. God is able! And all heaven will break loose when we do make those changes.

Possibly the greatest change we need deals with the subject of forgiveness. That is why I have devoted the next chapter to this important subject.

7

The Importance of Forgiveness

The first thing of which we must be certain is that because God is absolutely righteous and just at all times, we can never attach blame to Him, and therefore, we can never forgive Him. "He is the Rock, His work is perfect; for all His ways are justice, a God of truth and without injustice; righteous and upright is He" (Deuteronomy 32:4).

Many times, we can find ourselves in difficult situations where we cannot understand the justice of God, and we are tempted to doubt His unfailing love and perfect justice. Worse still, we can start believing God has failed us. The only way to navigate those turbulent waters related to our faith journey is to be firmly anchored in the Word of God's passages that relate to God's justice. "The LORD is just in all his ways, and kind in all his doings" (Psalm 145:17 RSV).

Because God knows the end from the beginning, He knows where He is taking us in order to bless us. That means we must trust Him where we cannot trace Him. And if we have resentment toward God, we need to repent of that sin. Sin hinders our close relationship with Him.

When we fully trust in God's flawless character, regardless of the circumstances, then we can fully worship and praise Him. That is where the action is!

In order for us to forgive people, they have to have been guilty of some offense toward us. We must not presume, however, that because we are feeling hurt, the people who hurt us were necessarily guilty of doing wrong. Let's take a look at some common reasons that we might feel hurt and be tempted toward resentment:

- We were not consulted.
- We were not included in some group situation.
- We were not spoken to by someone who we thought should acknowledge us.
- We were not given enough attention.
- We were not given recognition for things for which we were responsible.
- We were justly corrected by someone.

The more objectively we ponder these common circumstances, the more we can understand that in each case, the other people involved *could* have been innocent of wrongdoing.

So let's get real and ask God to reveal to us where our ego has been affected. Has our pride been the basic cause of our resentment toward people's actions, or lack of them? God may show us that in the area of our communications, we have been insensitive to others' needs. Let's look at some instances:

- Perhaps we have been insensitive to others' needs by unnecessary communication in the first place.
- Maybe we were out of order in communicating. Was it the responsibility of someone else?

- Did we communicate in the right timing? It never ceases to amaze me that so few people who make a phone call ever ask the other person if it is a convenient time to speak!
- Did we communicate with the right method?
- Did we have the right attitude and motive when we made the communication?

Before we judge others whose responses to our communications are less than what we expected, or less than what we thought we deserved, let's ask God to show us what He wants to teach us through all of this.

It is imperative that we understand that when others unjustly wrong us, forgiveness is not optional. We still must be obedient to God's Word. Jesus makes this very clear in Matthew 6:14–15: "For if you forgive men their trespasses, your heavenly Father will also forgive you. But if you do not forgive men their trespasses, neither will your Father forgive your trespasses." Ever need God's forgiveness? Of course we all do! Then we *must* forgive others in order for our greatest need to be met.

Another important reason we need to forgive others is that when we do not forgive, resentment takes over, which in time inevitably causes disunity. This, in turn, can become the biggest stumbling block that gets in the way of unbelievers coming to Christ. Whereas nothing attracts unbelievers to Christ more than when we are consistently living in love and harmony with all other believers (see John 17:23). Heavy implications.

The more we love in a relationship, the more we can be hurt, especially when it involves injustice. Our deepest pain comes from those who are the closest to us. Let's look at some of the categories of people who may have unjustly hurt us:

- Wives, husbands, parents, children, brothers, sisters and other relatives

- Friends and acquaintances
- People under our authority

We find a poignant illustration of the first category, family, in 2 Samuel 13:38–39. Absalom was King David's son who murdered his brother Amnon for raping his sister Tamar. "So Absalom fled and went to Geshur, and was there three years. And King David longed to go to Absalom. For he had been comforted concerning Amnon, because he was dead."

Verse 37 says, "And David mourned for his son [Absalom] every day." But David did not do anything to bring about unity in this broken relationship. A huge lesson here—David never confronted Absolom, disciplined him or pursued reconciliation.

Finally, Joab (one of David's leaders) and a wise woman from Tekoa were used to get the message through to David that he needed to invite Absalom back. That long story takes 23 verses to tell in 2 Samuel 14:1–23. Now, take note of how King David reacted: "And the king said, 'Let him return to his own house, but do not let him see my face.' So Absalom returned to his own house, but did not see the king's face" (verse 24).

Verse 28 says, "And Absalom dwelt two full years in Jerusalem, but did not see the king's face." Twice Absalom asked Joab to help him get an appointment with his father, David, all to no avail. After trying again, his request was finally granted. He explained that he wanted serious communication with his father (see verse 32). But sadly, when Absalom was then released and in David's presence, and when he had bowed down on his face before his father, the Bible says David kissed Absalom—a normal greeting in that culture—but there is still no record of fellowship between them. The result was that Absalom led a treasonous assault against David and "stole the hearts of the men of Israel" (2 Samuel 15:6), causing David to have to leave the city.

What a price to pay for not pursuing reconciliation!

Real forgiveness will always lead to fellowship. The absence of fellowship with his father was the breeding ground for the seeds of betrayal that came into Absalom's heart. David became the cause of this temptation.

God's Word addresses this sin of causing offense strongly in Matthew 18:7: "Woe to the world because of offenses! For offenses must come, but woe to that man by whom the offense comes!"

When speaking about the last days prior to the Second Coming of the Lord Jesus—which is this present era—Jesus predicted, "And then many will be offended, will betray one another, and will hate one another" (Matthew 24:10). In Mark 13:12 Jesus says, "Now brother will betray brother to death, and a father his child; and children will rise up against parents and cause them to be put to death."

All these horrific scenarios will occur because people will not pursue forgiveness, which would have freed them from resentment. And unforgiveness, if not dealt with, will produce horrible disunity leading to death. How we need to heed these warnings in God's Word.

We need to think about the need to forgive governments that have failed us and caused us harm. Nations can hurt us and those near and dear to us. Spiritual leaders can fail us and hurt us. People we have been teamed with in ministry can wound us.

Hannah is a classic example of how to react when a spiritual leader has failed us badly. In 1 Samuel 1 we have the story of Hannah, whose name means "grace." She was pouring out her heart silently to the Lord in the Temple because of her inability to have children. She vowed that if God gave her a son, she would give him back to the Lord to serve all his lifetime in the Temple of the Lord. Eli the priest saw her and wrongly judged her as being a drunken woman, so he rebuked her forcibly.

71

If ever a woman could have been tempted to let a spiritual leader know how far off he was in his discernment of truth, it was now! She could have felt justified in letting him know he had totally misjudged her. But Hannah had a humble heart, trusted in God's faithfulness to vindicate her and simply stated the facts. Then Eli prayed a prayer of blessing over her, with an assurance that God would say yes to her petition for a son.

How many times does our resentment toward a spiritual leader who has hurt or misjudged us unjustifiably hinder our ability to receive the many blessings God intended us to receive from that same leader? Humility makes the difference and does not hinder unity, because our choice will be to forgive, and God's future plans to bless will be the result.

Pray with me: "Oh God, please help us to really grasp this vital principle and apply it whenever needed. In Jesus' name, I believe, Amen."

Biblical Principles on How to Forgive

By now you are probably thinking, *I wish the author would give us some practical tips on how to appropriate these injunctions. And I wonder if she has ever had to work through all this stuff.*

Okay, I understand this reaction. Here comes what I have had to live through, many times, and have proved it works every time.

First, we must take seriously the warning God gives us from His Word about the need to follow through until we know we have forgiven those who have wronged us. "See to it that no one fail to obtain the grace of God; that no 'root of bitterness' spring up and cause trouble, and by it the many become defiled" (Hebrews 12:15 RSV).

We must realize that forgiveness is an act of our will. We have to *want* to forgive.

We must recognize that resentment is a strongly destructive force to our minds, souls, bodies and spirits. We can lose our anointing of the Spirit in our ministries, and our ministries altogether in time, if we do not deal with resentment scripturally. The more responsibilities we have, the more we are tempted to resent God for the price we have to pay related to our calling. We have the wrong perspective. The privilege of serving the Creator and Sustainer of the universe is always higher than the price.

If we are teachers of God's Word and the people do not respond to our teaching in the way we expect and want, we can resent them. No one wants to listen to an unanointed, angry preacher who resents his or her listeners. Food for thought.

It has been medically proven that resentment can produce a number of illnesses, some of which are high blood pressure, ulcers, rashes, headaches and arthritis, to name a few. In Proverbs 14:30 (RSV) we have this fact confirmed: "A tranquil mind gives life to the flesh, but passion [anger or resentment] makes the bones rot." Significant!

In one of the meetings where I spoke on this subject, there was a girl who was wondering why she was always sick. Then she was convicted by the Holy Spirit of resentment toward her mother. She repented during the service. God then spoke into her spirit, "Jeremiah 30:17." She had no clue what that verse was, but on looking it up, she found, "'For I will restore health to you and heal you of your wounds,' says the LORD." During a time of people sharing what God had spoken to them from the message on forgiveness, this teenager shared her story openly. All were blessed.

Resentment destroys companionship and fellowship. In the story Jesus told in Luke 15, the prodigal son's older brother lost all enjoyment of fellowship with his father and younger brother through resentment toward them both. Think about all the fun and camaraderie he missed at the party where everyone else was celebrating the wayward son's return home and having a great time—while he was wallowing in his misery of resentment outside, on his own. There is no real freedom, joy or peace until we have chosen to forgive.

Our prayers are ineffective until we forgive. Notice the link between forgiveness and praying in Matthew 6:12, as Jesus instructs His disciples how to pray. He says, "Forgive us our debts, as we forgive our debtors." Then again in verses 14–15, Jesus says, "For if you forgive men their trespasses, your heavenly Father will also forgive you. But if you do not forgive men their trespasses, neither will your Father forgive your trespasses." How many of our prayers go unanswered because we will not forgive?

Now notice the link between forgiving and having faith when we pray:

> "Take heed to yourselves. If your brother sins against you, rebuke him; and if he repents, forgive him. And if he sins against you seven times in a day, and seven times in a day returns to you, saying, 'I repent,' you shall forgive him."
> And the apostles said to the Lord, *"Increase our faith."*
> So the Lord said, "If you have faith as a mustard seed, you can say to this mulberry tree, 'Be pulled up by the roots and be planted in the sea,' and it would obey you."
>
> Luke 17:3–6, emphasis added

I knew a mature Christian woman who had been praying for years for her son-in-law to change. He had been very unkind to her daughter and her daughter's two little children. The woman heard me give this message on forgiveness and repented of resentment toward him. That was at 11:00 p.m. on a Thursday night in her home. On Saturday her son-in-law drove to her home from many miles away to ask her forgiveness, saying that the Holy Spirit had deeply convicted him of his cruelty as a husband and father, and he had repented. The woman asked, "When did this happen?"

"At 11:00 p.m. on Thursday night," he replied.

That is a God incidence, not a coincidence!

Galatians 5:6 says faith works through love. We need to make sure both of those factors are operating when we are praying for others. Every time. All the time.

The most powerfully releasing principle is to think of all for which God has forgiven us. "Let all bitterness, wrath, anger, clamor, and evil speaking be put away from you, with all malice. And be kind to one another, tenderhearted, forgiving one another, even as God in Christ forgave you" (Ephesians 4:31–32).

After Peter had denied Jesus three times, all Jesus had to do was to look at Peter with forgiveness and it melted him to repentance. And remember when Peter asked Jesus if forgiving someone seven times would be enough? Jesus' classic reply was, "No, seventy times seven." Why? Because forgiving others was a way of life with Him.

When Judas came to betray the Lord, Jesus' first response was to say, "*Friend*, why are you here?" (Matthew 26:50 RSV, emphasis added). Hardly the normal response to a betrayer. When Jesus was hanging on the cross in agony of mind, body, soul and spirit, becoming our sinbearer and Savior, He cried out, "Father, forgive them; for they know not what they do" (Luke 23:34 RSV). Forgiveness was His way of life.

You may be thinking, *That's truly amazing, but I'm not Jesus.*

Point understood and received. But Stephen, a disciple of Jesus who was stoned to death for preaching the truth, prayed to God, "Lay not this sin [of murder] to their charge" (Acts 7:60 KJV). Why? Because forgiveness was a way of life to him also. And we can make the same choices. "Even as Christ forgave you, so you also must do" (Colossians 3:13).

The following story, shared by Erick Schenkel, executive director of the *JESUS* Film Project, is as powerful as anything I know to illustrate what I have just stated. It is about Jesus' disciples *today* who have chosen to make forgiveness a way of life.

> There is a region on the African continent known for breeding radicalism, violence and terror. The people are 100 percent committed to their religion, hostile to the gospel and to Jesus. The resistance is so steadfast that Christian leaders say it's been 1,000 years since they have truly heard the gospel.
>
> A national Christian leader had a heart to reach them. He trained and mobilized a group of college students, who volunteered to carry the gospel. They knew they could die in the effort. The students prayed and fasted, loaded up a supply of DVDs of the life of "JESUS," as told in the gospel of Mark, in the people's language, and began the journey . . . ready to give their lives in service to the Lord. On arrival they were immediately detected. Religious leaders demanded: "Who are you? Why are you here? What are you doing?"
>
> The students answered, "We are here to tell you the good news!" "What good news?" a leader scoffed. The students replied: "The good news is Jesus, His power to heal and save." The religious leader said: "OK, then. I have a challenge for you. We have a man here who has been insane for many, many years. If your Jesus can heal this man, we will follow Him. But if your Jesus fails, you *must* convert and follow our religion."

Full of faith and courage, the students agreed, saying, "Give us this man." He acted insane, apparently demonically oppressed. All night the students prayed over him, read the Word and praised their Lord, commanding the demons to release him. One by one, the demons yielded to the power of the Word and the blood of the Lamb. By morning, there were none left. He was completely delivered.

The students cleaned him up, shaved and showered him, and cut his nails. They returned to the town and presented him to the leader who had issued the challenge. The impact of the transformation—a man now sane and grateful—proved too much for them to accept. They went back on their word, beat the students and drove them out of the town. They locked the man in a small room, commanding him to say nothing. But he could not stay silent. **As people would walk by his cell, he kept glorifying God, shouting out, "Jesus healed me! Jesus healed me!"**

The whole town came to know what had happened, of the power of Jesus. News made it back to the students. Still recovering from their wounds, the original four asked the ministry director if they could return to the town, this time with four more students. He agreed. They went for the center of town, to the large market, where they openly and loudly proclaimed the gospel. Thousands heard: "It is Jesus who healed this man, whom we proclaim to you today. Believe and be healed. Receive Him and be forgiven." As they preached, the students passed out hundreds of DVDs of the life of "JESUS."

Those religious leaders again stepped in. They had the students arrested and beaten, and this time, thrown into jail where they spent the night with six suspects of an internationally known terrorist group. The group's leader was crying out all night from back pain, pleading for help. From their cell the students reached out to him: "We have a powerful medicine. Jesus can heal you. But you need to believe, repent and give your life to Christ." He believed and the Lord healed him—a powerful witness to all. That radical leader and his five suspected terrorists all gave their lives to the Lord. Even the police officer who heard the testimony during the night—and saw the miracle—also believed.

The result: an underground church was born—where there had not been a single believer for 1,000 years. The church members included **a police officer who had beaten them, a man delivered from demons, six former terrorists, and their families!** That was three years ago. The ministry director recently visited this underground church. He said it was flourishing, having grown to 40 members. They are giving out the DVDs of the "JESUS" film, have asked for more, and are talking of planting a church!

All heaven had broken loose! What an incredible display of Trinity unity and repeated forgiveness that outwitted and defeated the enemy's power and plans. All glory to our triumphant King Jesus!

I cannot stress too strongly how vitally important this next truth is. We need to ask God to give us His supernatural ability to love and forgive everyone who has wronged us, and then to receive it by faith.

We cannot do it any other way. It is a miracle working of the Holy Spirit. "The love of God has been poured out in our hearts by the Holy Spirit who was given to us" (Romans 5:5). And, "Without faith it is impossible to please Him, for he who comes to God must believe that He is, and that He is a rewarder of those who diligently seek Him" (Hebrews 11:6). God does not say He rewards casual inquirers!

Now we thank God for any or all of the blessings He has brought to us through the person we need to forgive.

You may have been so severely wronged and so deeply wounded emotionally and/or physically that you cannot think of anything for which to be thankful about certain people. I can totally understand that, with all that I have heard over my lifetime. But the fact that you are reading this book right now, with all this proven truth, is enough cause for you to be thankful, even if that is all you can honestly come up with.

Next, we think of the needs of the people at the time that they did us wrong—the needs of their mind, body, soul and spirit. Could there be different factors in their childhood, or later in life, that contributed to their behavior toward us? If so, it will help our level of understanding about their actions. It is possible that even now their needs are greater than ours.

A very practical way of getting free and keeping free from all resentment is to ask God to give us opportunities to express His love to our offenders in both word and deed. Perhaps we could do something to help them in some practical way. God would show us what and how, if we ask Him. "But if anyone has the world's goods and sees his brother in need, yet closes his heart against him, how does God's love abide in him? Little children, let us not love in word or speech but in deed and in truth" (1 John 3:17–18 RSV).

Finally, become an intercessor for them. And only pray loving prayers for God to bless them, encourage them, comfort them, strengthen them and meet their deepest needs. It is impossible for anyone to pray sincerely and often, as Jesus taught us to do in Luke 6:27–28, and still remain in the bondage of resentment.

Very often, we find it most difficult to forgive ourselves. We think that if we flail ourselves verbally often and strongly enough because of our failures and wrongdoings, it will somehow cause

All Heaven Will Break Loose

our guilty feelings to cease. The truth is, doing that is an insult to God's wondrous grace and mercy if we have already honestly and sincerely repented of our sins before God and humbled ourselves in making restitution to others wherever possible and as God directs. God says that He puts our sins in the sea of His forgetfulness. (See Micah 7:19; Isaiah 43:25.)

Our part is to receive God's forgiveness and then forgive ourselves. Jesus said that we are to love our neighbors as ourselves. We must love what God loves and hate what God hates. God loves us; He only hates our sin. We must learn, therefore, to love ourselves and hate our sin.

God's truth from God's Word, thoroughly applied as we depend entirely on the Holy Spirit to do His mighty liberating work in us, will inevitably set us free to be forgivers.

The next chapter illustrates the greatest teamwork in dynamic action that I have found anywhere in the Bible.

8

Teamwork That Saved a Nation from Annihilation

This chapter centers around the lives of Esther and Mordecai. We read about them in the book of Esther in God's Word, and they give us a uniquely poignant example of successful teamwork, from which we can learn a lot.

One of the main reasons God links our lives and ministries together with others is so we can learn His principles of teamwork. Many times we do not understand teamwork or even think about it, but we need to think about it—especially as it relates to unity in the Body of Christ, for which there is such a tremendous need.

These ministry links we have with others are in categories according to God's sovereign purposes. Marriage is one such link, but there are others. God intends some of these ministry links to be for a lifetime, as, of course, marriage is intended to be. But sometimes even outside of marriage they are intended for a lifetime, as with Mordecai and Esther.

Most times, the greater the purposes God has in linking ministries together, the greater the length of time they will stay together. But not always. Elijah and the widow at Zarephath only shared three and a half years linked together in ministry. Jonathan and his armorbearer in 1 Samuel 14 had a much shorter period, but with historic results.

The success of Mordecai and Esther in their individual roles and ministries—in fact, their very survival—depended on their teamwork. Neither could ever have made it alone. God set it up that way. In other words, they could not have fulfilled their destinies without each other.

When God links lives and ministries together today to affect missions, as the lives of Mordecai and Esther affected a mission, His principles of teamwork are exactly the same. That is why today, we need to heed and learn from their lives. As Matthew 12:25 (NIV) says, "Every kingdom divided against itself will be ruined [and there are no exceptions] and every city or household divided against itself will not stand."

I do not know of two better examples in the whole of God's Word than Esther and Mordecai for illustrating the unity that Jesus prayed for in John 17. Now, that is a colossal statement to make, and I certainly have never heard anybody else make it. They may have, but I have not heard it. The more I have made a study of this amazing book of Esther, the more I am convinced that its main purpose is to show the unity that Esther and Mordecai lived by and the reasons why we should study their lives.

Other important reasons for this book are to show that God will always defend His chosen people, the Jews, when they seek Him, and that God responds powerfully to God-directed fasting and intercession. It also confirms the truth from God's Word that those who bless the Jews will in turn be blessed.

The Characteristics of Unity

Let's look at the characteristics of unity exemplified by this unique couple. The first, and undoubtedly the strongest, is humility. As I have already emphasized, we are only as united as we are humble. Period. Anywhere. Anytime. We are only as loving as we are humble. These two, Mordecai and Esther, are a marvelous example of two strong leaders with two strong personalities. They were strong characters who had the necessary humility of heart to know that they desperately needed one another and always would, because God had sovereignly linked their lives and ministries together for His eternal purposes.

From a human perspective, these were two of the most unlikely people ever to be chosen to play major roles in shaping a nation. Mordecai was a Jewish Benjamite, an exile; Esther was his orphaned cousin, whom he adopted. What an unusual mix. But like Mary, the mother of Jesus, when the unusual was spoken over her and she said, "Be it unto me, according to Your word," these two had the same heart attitude. "As for God, His way [and His choice] is perfect" (Psalm 18:30 NIV). Pride argues with God's choices about whom He puts on our team. Humility accepts them and fulfills those purposes with joy and thanksgiving.

Interdependence

Another characteristic of unity is interdependence. Mordecai and Esther never showed a sign of an independent spirit toward each other in all the record of their lives, even under the severest tests. As an adult, Esther never outgrew her heart attitude of humility toward Mordecai. She recognized there were many things that God taught her, and would continue to teach her, through her new parent and later, senior partner in ministry.

God encourages this humility in relation to natural parents and spiritual parents: "My son, keep your father's commandment, and forsake not your mother's teaching. Bind them on your heart always; tie them around your neck" (Proverbs 6:20–21 ESV). "Listen to your father who gave you life, and do not despise your mother when she is old" (Proverbs 23:22 ESV).

Mordecai, in turn, had the humility of heart to see that at times he needed to receive "the word of the Lord" through a woman, someone he had trained for years. Esther 4:17 shows his humility: "So Mordecai went his way and did according to all that Esther commanded him." I wonder how many men today would pass that test. Mordecai certainly did, and that is why we need to look closely at this most remarkable man's life.

In movies we have seen on the book of Esther, the main focus is Esther. But there is *no way* she could ever have done what she did and fulfilled the destiny she had without this equally remarkable man, Mordecai, from whom we have so much to learn.

Their interdependence was like a game of tennis or Ping-Pong. Two players have to participate equally, and the ball has to be moving constantly from one side of the table, or the court, to the other. God plays this out in linking ministries. He moves by the Spirit on both ministries He links together. He puts His visions, His burdens, His directions and His strategies on each of the players, often equally—back and forth, back and forth.

All of the players have to be obedient to God's promptings. That is abiding by the rules; that is following the Holy Spirit's promptings. But we are not to concern ourselves with the score; that is God's business. Mordecai and Esther could not have cared less what the score was; just that they were submitted to God and submitted to one another, in the fear of the Lord.

I was thinking about how this works out in my own life. I do not know a better illustration to give you than the numerous times when my precious husband, Jim, and I have been teamed together in personal witnessing to people who have had difficult worldview questions like, "Why did God ever create the universe?" or "Why doesn't God wipe out evil?" or "Why didn't God remove the devil?"

I can remember the two of us being in a multimillionaire's home in the Beverly Hills area of Hollywood. The owner, a Christian lady, had brought in a top world-class neurosurgeon who was not a Christian. She was trying to win this doctor to the Lord. She brought us in because she knew he would ask a lot of penetrating questions—and he did. He fired questions at us *rapidly*, one after another. He was not convinced that Jesus was the Son of God, or that he needed to be accountable to Him.

That brilliant man grilled us with deep questions at length, and I sat there absolutely reveling in two things . . . and marveling. There were times when the answers would come to me as clear as a bell. I had no doubt about them and would speak them forth with conviction and authority, and the man knew it was truth. Then he would ask another question and I would go blank. I would not have a clue how to answer it. Immediately, the Holy Spirit would give Jim the perfect answer, and he would speak it with equal authority. God was playing His game of Ping-Pong or tennis between the two of us, and it did not matter to Jim or me who had the answers. We were both submitted to the Holy Spirit and were interdependent on one another. We just wanted the man to have the truth.

We have seen the same principles operating when we have been teamed together witnessing in all kinds of situations outdoors, such as at the Olympic Games here in America and in other nations around the world. Both of us were submitted to the Holy Spirit and were assured that we trusted each other as team partners. It was thrilling and fulfilling.

Recognizing God-Given Authority

Let's go on now to see more about Esther and Mordecai. When God catapulted Esther out of obscurity into great prominence and gave her another person in authority over her, her husband the king, she still remained submitted to her first God-given spiritual authority, Mordecai. We read about that in Esther 2:20: "Now Esther had not revealed her family and her people, just as Mordecai had charged her, for Esther obeyed the command of Mordecai as when she was brought up by him." We need to recognize our categories of authority and function in them at all times.

I will give you an illustration from my life. Any time I was in a situation where Jim was with me and I was speaking at a conference, which is mainly where I spoke, or in a church setting, I was automatically under three authorities. First of all was God, to whom I will answer at the Judgment Seat, and nobody else. I am most accountable to Him. Then I was accountable to Jim, my husband, as the spiritual head of our home. And then I was accountable and submitted to the authority of the people who brought me in to speak.

You might say, "I'm a single person, and I don't have a husband."

Then perhaps through a combination of people at different places and different times, God will place loving spiritual authority in your life. Ask Him to give you a community of friends, a place of belonging, and simply be obedient to the promptings of the Holy Spirit. In every situation, God will provide spiritual protection for you.

Now let's look at Mordecai. He did not pursue the fulfillment of his role and ministry without recognizing his link with Esther. So where do we find him when Esther is already in the palace, preparing for the beauty contest? He is not at home. We find him sitting at the king's gate so he can be in close contact with his God-given ministry link. And while he was there, God gave him the platform for his promotions. We see this in Esther 2:21. In verse 22, Mordecai discovered the secret plot about the threat to the king's life, but he did not act independently and try to see the king himself. He could have thought, *I'm going to get the credit for this, and I'll do everything I can to get through to the king and let him know that I'm the one who's going to save his life!* No, Mordecai recognized that Esther had access to the king that he did not have, and he used her God-given role of influence and their unique relationship to get the message through about the treason that was planned. This recognition is significant.

Esther, in turn, obeyed Mordecai. Watch the ball moving from one court to the other as they remain in God's callings, submitted to the Holy Spirit, in obedience to His promptings, in interdependence of relationship with one another. Esther obeyed Mordecai and gave the king the message "crediting Mordecai with the information"—those are the words in *The Living Bible*. And verse 23 in the Revised Standard Version tells us, "And it was recorded in the Book of the Chronicles in the presence of the king."

What is God saying to us? He has the perfect record of every ministry that has functioned behind the scenes. Behind the scenes, people have played a vital and sometimes crucial role in relation to all of our ministries. People may not have recorded it, but God has, and one day all will be known.

Luke 12:2 (ESV) says, "Nothing is covered up that will not be revealed, or hidden that will not be known." The less we cover up now about how others are used of God in our lives, the less embarrassed we will be at the Judgment Seat, where all will be disclosed.

The teamwork between Esther and Mordecai saved the king's life, and the enemies of the king were destroyed. What is God saying to us? God's Kingdom will always be advanced and

Satan's forces destroyed when we operate on the greatest levels of humility and honesty.

Honoring Our Ministry Links

I am always glad to have the opportunity of honoring my wonderful father and mother, who undoubtedly had the strongest influence in my life in relation to my fulfilling my destiny. I delight to honor this godly couple who are in heaven. Remarkable parents!

And I want to honor my precious husband, Jim, recently gone to be with the Lord. There is no way in a million years that I ever could have done what I have, submitted to the Lordship of Jesus and in the power of the Holy Spirit, without Jim. In our later years, most of his ministry was behind the scenes. I desperately needed him and his input in my life, all the time—a faithful, wonderful partner, prayer partner, best friend, lover of worship and of God's Word. He was also a remarkable father, grandfather and great-grandfather.

When I think of all the intercessors who have prayed for me, the secretaries who have helped me and the donors who have faithfully given to us (Jim and I have lived entirely by faith, never having had a salary in the last 42 years), I think of how much I owe to them all and how I long for them to be honored. Perhaps that deep desire will be fulfilled when we all stand before the Judgment Seat of Christ.

And then a special honor goes to my dear brother in the Lord Loren Cunningham, pioneer and founder of YWAM, who found me in New Zealand and released my ministry to the nations. I also honor those who have invited me to speak anywhere at any time; they are those who have recognized and released my ministry. How I honor those with whom God has linked me as team members in ministry and in friendship!

Lastly, I honor the authors who have written deep truths from God's Word. God has used them to shape my life in a profound way. How much I owe to them.

Now back to Esther and Mordecai. They recognized and deeply respected each other's divine calling and different ministry functions, and they saw how they completed each other. They also understood the insanity of competing with each other. Romans 12:9–10 (NIV) says, "Love must be sincere. Hate what is evil; cling to what is good. Be devoted to one another in love. Honor one other above yourselves." These two exemplified those truths and were completely devoid of competitiveness and jealousy. This is when teamwork becomes exhilarating, exciting, fulfilling and extremely successful.

I think of Loren Cunningham when I think of being teamed in public ministry. What a privilege! For decades, always with other YWAM staff or other international speakers, we went around the world, speaking at spiritual leadership conferences. We also ministered in refugee camps in such places as Cambodia, Thailand and Hong Kong. Together we led significant moves of God's Spirit among hundreds of people within YWAM and outside of it.

In numerous nations where the Holy Spirit would show us that there was to be application of our teaching, it could involve leading hours of intercession over nations. The Spirit of God would sovereignly come upon Loren, and he would know exactly how to lead a group into the next phase of praying together. And then I would know exactly where to take up from there and lead the next move of God's Spirit. . . . And so it would go on like that at length, without any human conferring. That is the kind of teamwork we see in the lives of Esther and Mordecai. There is no competition in it, but a lot of honoring and preferring one another.

I remember a time in Denver, Colorado, on a Sunday evening in Dr. Charles Blair's church. Loren and I had been speaking all week at a spiritual leadership conference. This night, Loren was the speaker, and I was sitting in the front row with the rest of the team. Loren was speaking on the subject of forgiveness. He had been speaking for about twenty-five minutes when he stopped and looked down at me and said, "Joy, you've got some powerful points helping people to get through to forgiveness. Why don't you just come up here and give them?" I did just that for about twelve minutes and sat down, and on we went. We could even team teach together!

The most remarkable experience of teamwork in my lifetime took place in Hartford, Connecticut. Loren Cunningham, Campbell McAlpine and I were teamed together speaking at a spiritual leadership conference. It took four pages in the revised edition of my book *Intimate Friendship with God* (Chosen, 2008) to record this most unusual and truly awesome account of teamwork, which took place over three days. Since you can read about it there, I will not relay it here, except to say that only God could have possibly orchestrated it all, including its mighty outworkings.

Team Testing

The next thing we see about Esther and Mordecai is that their unity was severely tested. The longer we are meant to be together and the greater the purposes for our being a team, the greater the testing will be. Marriage, of course, is the greatest test of all.

Esther 3 tells us about a major attack from an enemy, Haman, who came to destroy thousands of Jewish lives, including the lives of Mordecai and Esther. Through this major attack, their teamwork was tested in new ways.

We always need to inquire of God as to the purpose of an attack. If there is a continuous attack of the enemy on any relationship, we need to seek God until He reveals the cause, because Proverbs 16:7 says, "When a man's ways please the

LORD, He makes even his enemies to be at peace with him."
An important point.

In teamwork our motives can be tested, especially when we
are in obscurity and our partner is operating publicly. Mordecai
certainly passed that test. He was in obscurity for the first five
chapters of Esther. That is a lot of obscurity! It didn't bother
him a bit.

There are also tests we face in public ministry that we do
not face when in obscurity. These tests come when we are more
at the forefront. We have added responsibilities and are tested
to see whether we will discharge them in the fear of the Lord,
according to the ways of God. This can involve a lot of time
spent seeking God about a lot of things. And it means being
completely released from the fear of man. God tests us to see
how we will react to the inevitable criticisms that come when
we are out there in the front, in leadership.

Mordecai passed all his tests; he refused to pay homage to
Haman even though he knew this would enrage the man. When
God gave Mordecai the initial knowledge that Haman was ma-
nipulating things to condemn the Jews, what did he do? He
came out of obscurity and publicly led his people in fasting
and mourning. There is so much to learn from Mordecai's life!

Esther in turn made it her business to find out the cause
of Mordecai's distress. She didn't say, "Well now, I am in the
palace—I can't be concerned with his problems." No way! She
sincerely wanted to know what was going on with her cousin.
This team teaches us that without fellowship, there is no real
ministry function. Fellowship requires communication. So much
disunity is caused through lack of communication or unclear
communication.

"If there is any encouragement in Christ, any incentive of
love, any participation in the Spirit, any affection and sympathy,
complete my joy by being of the same mind, having the same

love, being in full accord and of one mind" (Philippians 2:1–2 RSV). The more we look into all the things stated in this passage, the more we see that they require clear communication.

Esther and Mordecai learned to "subject [themselves] to one another out of reverence for Christ" (Ephesians 5:21 RSV). What an important verse! This was vividly demonstrated in Esther 4 as they magnificently passed the next test of giving and receiving strong direct communication with each other under pressured and in difficult circumstances. Wow. Let's look at it. Mordecai shared with Esther the plan the king had issued for annihilating the Jews, and with it, a strong directive for her next move. He told her to go to the king and petition him on their behalf. No messing around—the lives of the Jews were at stake!

Esther in turn (watch the ball go from one side of the court to the other), under terrific pressure, responded by telling Mordecai her plight: "If I do as you say, I could die" (see Esther 4:11). How direct can communication get?

Mordecai's famous authoritative response was,

"Do not think in your heart that you will escape in the king's palace any more than all the other Jews. For if you remain completely silent at this time, relief and deliverance will arise for the Jews from another place, but you and your father's house will perish. Yet who knows whether you have come to the kingdom for such a time as this?"

Esther 4:13–14

Esther responded with an equally famous authoritative directive to him. I love it. Verse 16—in my paraphrased version—says, "You get a lot of Jews to fast and pray for me, and I and my maids will do the same. Then I'll go to the king, against the law, and do as you say, even if I die doing it."

Then verse 17 says, "So Mordecai went his way and did according to all that Esther commanded him."

Those are strong directives back and forth. The Holy Spirit was giving them their answers as they were submitting to one another in the fear of the Lord. Fabulous!

We need to have the humility of heart to receive counsel, directions and exhortations from those with whom God has teamed us. Notice I included *directions* because I am coming up with an illustration for this. My classic example is out of my own life because I want you to know that these truths are not coming from theory. They are coming from my having lived them in the power of the Holy Spirit and in the fear of the Lord, which is the only way they can be lived.

All week long I had been teaching at a spiritual leadership conference at YWAM's University of the Nations campus in Kona, Hawaii. It came to Thursday evening, when all of the many schools, plus all of the staff and teachers, come together for a communal meeting. Outside visitors also come to the campus for the meeting. One of the outside speakers from the many spheres of training brought in for that week would be the speaker, and I knew this would be my responsibility. All day long, from the first minute I opened my eyes on that Thursday morning until the evening, I sought the face of God diligently to know what "the word of the Lord" was that I was to speak to the whole community. I never went outside the bedroom door, but no answers were coming to me.

I was listening in silence, reading the Word of God, interceding for others; I was coming against the enemy and doing spiritual warfare, thanking God, praising Him and worshiping Him. There was not anything else I knew to do. Then it came to around 6:00 p.m. and I still was thinking, *It will come any minute.* Nothing.

Finally, I got a message through to Loren Cunningham, our leader, saying that I needed to speak to him. It took some time before he was able to get to me; he was thinking, of course, that I had a message to speak. I said to him, "I've sought God diligently all day, but I don't have a clue what I'm supposed to do tonight. All I know to do is say, 'Will you pray for me?' Maybe I'll get it then—because that has happened in the past."

Loren prayed earnestly for me, and we both expected the message title would come to me while we waited in silence. . . . Nothing.

Then Loren took on his role of responsibility, knowing that the ball was totally back in his court since there was nothing more I could do. He and I both knew that I would never, ever give anything other than what the Holy Spirit gave me to speak on specifically at a particular time. That was a given! So Loren sought the Lord earnestly to see what he was to do. Maybe he was to speak? Maybe somebody else? Maybe he was to turn it into some other kind of meeting? My role was then to intercede for him, which I did.

By this time the meeting had actually started, the worship had begun and we still did not know what we were going to do. Loren kept seeking God diligently. He is big and tall, and I am small. Finally he looked down at my five-foot-one frame and gave me a directive by saying, "You are to preach the Gospel." I felt immediately the witness of the Spirit to this instruction. I had no time to prepare; I had not a clue how I was going to present the Gospel, but I knew it was one of the tests of teamwork. I just said, "Okay! I will."

As the worship continued, I lifted my heart to God and said, "How do I do it?" These thoughts came into my mind from Jeremiah 9:23–24 (verses I was very familiar with):

> Thus says the LORD: "Let not the wise man glory in his wisdom, let not the mighty man glory in his might, nor let the rich man glory in his riches; but let him who glories glory in this, that he understands and knows Me, that I am the LORD, exercising lovingkindness, judgment, and righteousness in the earth. For in these I delight," says the LORD.

94

The Holy Spirit then said, "Preach the Gospel on the basis of My character; explain who I am from these three verses." And then He flashed into my mind Romans 10:9–10 (RSV),

> If you confess with your lips that Jesus is Lord and believe in your heart that God raised him from the dead, you will be saved. For man believes with his heart and so is justified, and he confesses with his lips and so is saved.

I only had time to send up a telegram prayer asking God to anoint me, declaring that without Him I could do nothing, when it was announced that I would speak. I was out "walking on the water," cast upon God, who never fails. After quoting Jeremiah 9:23–24, I said that I did not know a better commercial for God's character in all of God's Word than those verses—and I took off explaining each of those three main attributes. Then I preached on making Jesus Lord of our lives and the need to publicly say it with our mouths if we have made that transaction. As a response to the appeal, fourteen people openly and boldly declared Jesus as Lord for the first time in their lives.

That response was worth everything God had required of me that whole day and evening! And God has never put me through that particular test again.

Often, leaders act defensively when someone shares with them a directive, a warning, a revelation or some vision about the ministry. It seems as if they feel the need to convey that they are the ones who bring the initial directives; otherwise, they think it might look as if they have failed in their leadership. That is sad. Leaders particularly need to understand at a deeper level that they were never meant to have all the vision and revelation related to ministry purposes, because no one is meant to have it all. God evenly distributes it out to others so that we may be interdependent on Him through one another.

Honoring Others

Another warning to leaders is the need to recognize, release and report God's directives through others. King Jehoshaphat did this magnificently in 2 Chronicles 20:14–15, in a time of great crisis when he did not know what to do but was looking to the Lord. Then it says in verse 14, "The Spirit of the LORD came upon Jahaziel," who was a Levitical priest out in the crowd. He was not a leader. As soon as Jahaziel delivered the word of the Lord, King Jehoshaphat immediately recognized it, fell on his face before the Lord in worship and later exhorted all the people to believe in the Lord and to believe in the prophet who gave them their directions.

Paul is a shining example of a ministry leader who lived what I am sharing with you. In Romans 13:7 (RSV) he says to pay "honor to whom honor is due." Romans 16 is one of my favorite chapters. You may wonder why since it is just a list of all the people Paul worked with at that time in his life. That is exactly why. It is a long list honoring his team members one by one, because he knew he could not possibly have done what he did without each of them. We seldom hear this today when a leader is interviewed about the ministry God has entrusted to him or her.

We now look at how Esther and Mordecai passed the test of having to get directions and timing from God alone. As they remained interdependent upon one another, these two remarkable people teach us so many lessons about total dependence on God, with humility and the fear of the Lord. In Esther 5, the public focus shifted heavily to Esther as she risked her life for her people; while Mordecai was *always* cooperating in conjunction with her. He worked diligently behind the scenes, organizing prayer and fasting. Now Esther had to get the blueprint from God directly for the wisest way of presenting her very difficult case before the king. God was testing her ability to depend on Him alone in a crisis situation when she could not get to Mordecai.

At these times when there is no one else but God, the truth of the following Scriptures comes alive to us: "All my springs are in you" (Psalm 87:7), and "You are complete in Him" (Colossians 2:10). We are to cast ourselves upon Him and know that *He will not fail us*, as He promises to direct us in Psalm 32:8 (RSV): "I will instruct you and teach you the way you should go, I will counsel you with my eye upon you."

Conversely, God can be testing us by withholding from us what we are to do, to see whether we will call for help. And through the prayers of others, the answer will come to us. I have been tested on that one, and by His grace I have passed the test on several occasions.

Back to Esther. She proved her sensitivity to the restraint of the Spirit by not bringing her request to the king until there was a full release in her spirit to do so. She understood Ecclesiastes 8:5–6 (RSV), "He who obeys a command will meet no harm, and the mind of a wise man will know the time and way. For every matter has its time and way. . . ."

How many times God's purposes are aborted because we do not discipline our lives to seek God in detail, or we disobey His restraint in our spirits or do not heed His warnings. How that can mess us up.

Back to Mordecai. When Haman was in the process of being found out and actually had to go through the streets himself and give Mordecai the ultimate VIP treatment, we note that this publicity and honor did not affect Mordecai a bit. Esther 6:12 (RSV) says, "Then Mordecai returned to the king's gate [not to his house]." Why did he sit outside the king's gate? Because Esther was inside the gate, in the king's palace. No matter how prominent he had become, he still saw his need to be as near to her as possible.

Later, chapter 7 focuses dramatically back on Esther as she uncompromisingly makes her request for her nation and boldly exposes the enemy Haman. As a result, in chapter 8 verse 1 she was given Haman's house and was rewarded by the king. But Esther knew what God knew. *The defeat of the enemy was the result of teamwork.* Esther honored Mordecai in front of the king and told him what she owed to Mordecai. Aren't these two a phenomenal team? Such beautiful humility!

A high price comes with higher privileges of leadership. That is what God was bringing these two to—both of them feared God and not men and were obedient to God's directives, even if it meant the cost of their lives. And both paid a high price to lead. They led through their respective ministry functions. The early Church worked this way, never from leadership positions, as I shared in chapter 6.

Maturity for the Purpose of Evangelism

The mission of Esther and Mordecai was always saving life that the enemy had planned to destroy. Our greatest goal and deepest point of unity must always be to see the Body of Christ strengthened, that the lost may be saved. Paul lived this in a tremendous way. He says in Colossians 1:28–29 (RSV), "Him [Jesus] we proclaim, warning every man and teaching every man in all wisdom, that we may present every man mature in Christ. For this I toil, striving with all the energy which he mightily inspires within me." He is writing about bringing the Body of Christ to full maturity. Out of the same heart, Paul writes in 1 Corinthians 9:16 (RSV), "Woe to me if I do not preach the gospel!" So many times we see ministries majoring in one or the other—either bringing the Body to maturity or preaching the Gospel. It is not one or the other. It is both!

In my diligent preparation of this particular chapter, the Holy

Spirit directed me strongly to emphasize evangelism. Listen to the importance Jesus placed on it in His life. In John 18:37 (ESV) He said, "For this purpose I have come into the world—to bear witness to the truth." Surely, our purpose should be to do the same—witness to others that Jesus is the Way, the Truth and the Life. Jesus said, "Follow Me, and I will make you fishers of men" (Matthew 4:19).

If we are not witnessing to others as a way of life, we are not fully following Him. That is loaded in its implications. When did you last witness about your faith? When did you last lead a soul to Christ? Is it even a part of your life, let alone a way of life?

"But you shall receive power when the Holy Spirit has come upon you; and you shall be witnesses to Me . . . to the end of the earth [wherever you go]" (Acts 1:8). If we are not witnessing to those who do not know Jesus about what He has done to transform our lives, we are not fulfilling the main purpose for being empowered by the Holy Spirit. In the natural, we are usually born to reproduce life. We are reborn into God's family to reproduce souls in the power of the Holy Spirit, through a burdened heart for the lost, in interceding for them as a way of life and in witnessing to them as a way of life. Otherwise, we are barren.

We need to get desperate before God and ask Him to give us a fresh revelation of the horrendous reality of hell. Here is a little stanza of a song I used to sing a lot in New Zealand, before we came to America, which has been deeply imprinted onto my life, my soul and my spirit:

> Lost sinners are dying in darkness today,
> and so few seem willing to show them the way,
> oh give me a passion and vision I pray,
> make me a winner of souls.

Under the Spirit's control
Father please give me a soul,
lead me I pray, to someone today,
make me a winner of souls.

The above has been a repeated lifetime prayer of mine, and out of it has come a life of personal soul-winning, in the power of the Holy Spirit.

Jesus stood up in the synagogue and said,

"The Spirit of the LORD is upon Me, because He has anointed Me to preach the gospel to the poor; He has sent Me to heal the brokenhearted, to proclaim liberty to the captives and recovery of sight to the blind, to set at liberty those who are oppressed; to proclaim the acceptable year of the LORD."

Luke 4:18–19

According to Jesus' life and teaching, any ministry that does not include a vision and a burden for lost souls is totally unbalanced. I cannot find any time where Jesus says, "Come into the synagogue and listen to Me tell you the truth." Almost all of Jesus' personal evangelism was done out in the marketplace, where people were. Think about that. Remember, Jesus is our model. To become fishers of men, we need to go fishing where the fish are, and they are *out there* in the marketplace. It means going out and gossiping the Gospel.

Jesus sent the disciples out two by two, into the towns and villages, and said in Matthew 10:7–8, "And as you go, preach, saying 'The kingdom of heaven is at hand.' Heal the sick, cleanse the lepers, raise the dead, cast out demons. Freely you have received, freely give." This is obviously a power evangelism mandate. Not to have the power demonstrated amongst the people is shortchanging them of the Gospel. The implications of that are heavy.

Evangelism was not intended as an event, but as a way of life. It should be as natural as eating and sleeping. It was a way of life in the home I was brought up in. It was absolutely normal to see my parents sharing their faith with everyone God brought across their paths.

Let me give you an illustration of how normal witnessing should and can be. I had been speaking at a leadership conference throughout the week in an overseas country. It was a Saturday, and Jim and I were walking through a beautiful city park, interceding for the nation we were in at that time. Then I saw a man walking in front of us who appeared to be in his thirties or forties. Immediately, I felt that familiar little nudge from the Holy Spirit that I was to witness to him. I walked toward him, totally depending on the Holy Spirit, softly saying, "Thank You, Lord, that You will give me the right words."

When I got up to the man, smiling and relaxed, I said, "Excuse me, sir, my husband and I are just walking in the park, and we are praying for this nation. I noticed you in front of us, and I had an impression that I was to come up to you and ask two simple questions: 'Have you problems in your life right now that seem unsolvable? And are there burdens you are carrying that are heavy, for which you need help?' Because I believe God has the answer to your problems. Does this make any sense to you?"

"Oh," he said, "does it ever!" By this time Jim had joined me and stood quietly praying for God to work. "As a matter of fact," the man said, "I'm sick in my body, I've recently lost my job and I have no idea where I can get employment. I'm very concerned about where the money will come from to pay the rent on my apartment. I'm very lonely, and I was just walking in this park saying to myself, *Well, I haven't been to church for a while, and I think I'll give up on God.*"

Could anything have been more coordinated in bringing two people together . . . just a Christian doing what was a way of life, obeying a prompting of the Holy Spirit to approach another person? As we stood there in the quiet and privacy of those spacious grounds, I was able to pray in faith for the man's body to be healed. Jim gave him the money in that country's currency that was in his pocket. Then I was able to say to the man, "I have been speaking at a conference this last week at a church very near here." It was less than half a mile from where we were walking. I was able to point to it. He knew the church, although he had not been to it. I was able to tell him it was full of wonderful, friendly Christian people. I said, "I will guarantee you that because of this encounter with each other today, which is obviously a God setup, if you will put God back into your life and go to that church next Sunday and share your needs with the pastoral staff, your needs will start to be met. Return to God, and return to fellowshiping with His people."

The man said that without question, this was a God setup. He declared with conviction that he was returning to God and would be going to that church next week. Hallelujah.

I could give numerous other illustrations of my witnessing all around the world that are much more dramatic, but I chose that story to show how normal, natural and easy it is to witness to others when we are submitted and obedient to the Holy Spirit and when we make witnessing a way of life.

Submission to Authority

Back to Esther and Mordecai. After all that had taken place, both were submitted to the king, who had the final authority. They never operated outside of that authority, manifesting humility and the fear of the Lord. Very significant. After passing all of those tests, they could have thought, *Well, now we're going to do our own thing*. Not this team. Because of their submission to the king, he then gave them greater riches and greater authority.

God only releases greater privileges and authority to us today as we are submitted to the authorities whom He puts over us.

And they do not have to be perfect. King Xerxes was not necessarily perfect. We do not know about his life and character, but he was the headship over Esther and Mordecai.

Remember that Saul was anything but a perfect leader. He was filled with jealousy toward David, but David was very aware of God's admonition "Do not touch My anointed ones, and do My prophets no harm" in Psalm 105:15. This admonition needs to be taken very seriously.

"He who fears God shall come forth from them all" (Ecclesiastes 7:18 RSV). We see it with David, and we see it with Esther and Mordecai. Esther passed the life-or-death test the second time because she went to the king twice without being summoned. After that second time, the king told her the most amazing thing: She could ask again. Anything she requested, he said, would be granted her.

When we have the humility of heart and fear of the Lord, when teamed with other ministries, to fulfill these principles of unity, and when we are prepared to spend part of our lives in intercession for nations and people who are in spiritual death, then God will sovereignly take the initiative with us and say, "Ask what you want today." He will do it.

It is an absolutely awesome experience. How do I know? One day God spoke to me three times from three different places in His Word and said, "This day, as an intercessor, ask anything you want of Me and I will give it to you." It only happened once, and I had two spiritual leaders in the room with me to witness it. One was my husband.

Every single one of my seven requests was related to the expansion of God's Kingdom worldwide. I have lived at 87 to see many of them being answered.

Finally, we see the immense privilege given to Esther and Mordecai of being prototypes for future generations. In chapter 9, they functioned publicly together in their ministries and leadership roles, giving directives to both present and future generations as they established Purim. This was two days set aside to recall and rejoice over the way that God had used these two ministries to lead a nation from destruction to freedom.

We only reach the lost in the nations that God has placed us in, and in the other nations, when we have this kind of vision and a commitment to God and to each other in teamwork. Are we modeling up front, where all can see, this kind of unity?

Jesus paid the biggest price ever to leave a comfort zone and fulfill a destiny. In the next chapter, we are invited to leave our comfort zones and go to the nations, to do our part in helping see that they fulfill their destinies. In doing so, we will find that we are fulfilling ours.

9

Teamwork That Won a War

First Samuel 14 tells a remarkable story of two young men in the hands of God who accomplished an amazing military victory. They are also a classic example of what can be done when operating on the biblical principles of unity.

Introducing Jonathan and his armorbearer. I would love to know the armorbearer's name to honor him, but we are not told what it was. Jonathan would be familiar with the Old Testament concept described in Zechariah 4:10, which says that we are not to despise the day of small beginnings. He believed that one man and God are already a majority. With his armorbearer as a partner, that was an even greater majority!

Jonathan believed similarly to Isaiah: "Behold, I will do a new thing, now it shall spring forth; shall you not know it? I will even make a road in the wilderness and rivers in the desert" (Isaiah 43:19). He believed that God is ingenious in His creativity, delights in doing new things and is limitless in power. "Ah, Lord GOD! Behold, You have made the heavens and the earth

All Heaven Will Break Loose

by Your great power and outstretched arm. There is nothing too hard for You" (Jeremiah 32:17).

Jonathan also believed that to gain significant breakthrough in victory over territory that Satan had under his control, he and his partner would have to move out of all their comfort zones. They would have to be prepared for the unpredictable to become the normal.

Unfortunately, the majority of God's people either do not believe these concepts or are not prepared to act on them when the Holy Spirit releases vision. God's Word proves it. The history of the Church proves it. People prefer to stay within their comfort zones. But not this pioneering minority plus God! Let's see how they lived out what they believed.

"Now it happened one day that Jonathan the son of Saul said to the young man who bore his armor, 'Come, let us go over to the Philistines' garrison that is on the other side.' But he did not tell his father" (1 Samuel 14:1). The reason he did not tell was because his earthly leader and father was King Saul, who was a disobedient, unanointed man. Wisely, Jonathan never shared his vision, knowing it would have been squashed. He did not act in rebellion, though. An important point.

First Samuel 13:14 says that God had already dismissed Saul as leader over Israel and appointed David. Saul, the present military leader, was seated at his command center with six hundred men, without any battle plan in mind. There was no evidence of God's directions to him.

Here is where we see the start of the formidable challenges that went with the enormous opportunities facing these two young men, Jonathan and his armorbearer. The armies of the Israelites and the Philistines occupied high positions facing each other but were separated by an extremely deep, rugged ravine. The challenges to Jonathan and his armorbearer were in the form of two large, dangerous, sharp rocks. One was called Bozez,

106

meaning slippery. The other was called Seneh, meaning thorny. (See 1 Samuel 14:4.) The Philistines never dreamed that anyone in his right mind would attempt to climb them bare-handed, and then attempt to fight after that feat!

These slippery, thorny and dangerous rocks represent some of the exploits that have yet to be done to overcome Satan's strongholds in the lives of millions yet to be reached with the Gospel. "The people who know their God shall stand firm and take action" (Daniel 11:32 RSV). Young, willing warriors, with God, will do exploits that have never been done in the history of the Church.

First Samuel 14:6 tells us why Jonathan and his armorbearer could be so outrageously bold and daring: "Then Jonathan said to the young man who bore his armor, 'Come let us go over to the garrison of these uncircumcised; it may be that *the LORD will work for us.* For nothing restrains the LORD from saving by many or by few'" (emphasis added).

What an extravagant statement of faith! Their confidence was *solely* in God. They knew that for God to get all the glory, it may well be that God had planned to work through few rather than many. Jonathan would remember how God had done that with Gideon and his whittled-down number of three hundred men to defeat the Midianites, the Amalekites and the people of the East. Judges 6:5 says these enemies were "as numerous as locusts, both they and their camels were without number." God revealed that the purpose of Gideon's team being so small at the time was "lest Israel claim glory for itself against Me, saying, 'My own hand has saved me'" (Judges 7:2). As God said in Isaiah 42:8, "My glory I will not give to another."

Malachi 2:1–2 (RSV) gives us an understanding of God's reactions when we rob Him of His glory: "And now, O priests, this command is for you. If you will not listen, if you will not lay it to heart to give glory to my name, says the LORD of hosts, then . . . I will curse your blessings."

A wonderful hymn by Kittie Louise Suffield says, "Little is much when God is in it!" How true. Conversely, if your plan does not originate with God—forget it.

The next secret to the success of these two young men is found in 1 Samuel 14:7, "So his armorbearer said to him, 'Do all that is in your heart. Go then; here I am with you, according to your heart.'" The pioneering minority plus God were in total unity, through a mutually shared vision, total trust, total support of each other and relying totally on God. Verse 8 shows there was no independent spirit operating in this team: "Then Jonathan said, 'Very well, let *us* cross over to these men, and *we* will show ourselves to them'" (emphasis added).

Another major factor in the success of their daring exploits was that they made certain it was the will and purpose of God before going any farther. They inquired of the Lord, as Gideon did. Verses 9–10 (emphasis added) say,

> "If they say thus to us, 'Wait until we come to you,' then we will stand still in our place and not go up to them. But if they say thus, 'Come up to us,' then we will go up. For the LORD has delivered them into our hand and *this will be a sign to us.*"

God loves it when we ask for confirmation or correction to make sure we are not acting in presumption. Presumption is a prevalent, grievous sin. David knew the high price he had paid in his leadership for this sin. That is why he prayed in Psalm 19:13, "Keep back your servant also from presumptuous sins; let them not have dominion over me. Then I shall be blameless, and I shall be innocent of great transgression."

Listen to the heart cry of God in Psalm 81:11–14,

> But My people would not heed My voice, and Israel would have none of Me. So I gave them over to their own stubborn heart,

to walk in their own counsels. Oh, that My people would listen to Me, that Israel would walk in My ways! I would soon subdue their enemies, and turn My hand against their adversaries.

How many times have God's purposes been thwarted in people's lives because they have not waited long enough to hear God's directions?

First Samuel 14:11 says of these two young men, "*Both* of them showed themselves to the garrison of the Philistines" (emphasis added). Again, no spirit of independence in this team.

- We are only as strong as we are united. "Every city or house divided against itself will not stand" (Matthew 12:25).
- We are only as united as we are loving. "Fulfill my joy by being like-minded, having the same love, being of one accord, of one mind" (Philippians 2:2).
- We are only as loving as we are humble. "With all lowliness . . . bearing with one another in love . . . keep the unity of the Spirit in the bond of peace" (Ephesians 4:2–3).

The young men's story goes on: "And the Philistines said, 'Look, the Hebrews are coming out of the holes where they have hidden.' Then the men of the garrison called to Jonathan and his armorbearer, and said, 'Come up to us, and we will show you something'" (1 Samuel 14:11–12). God's sign of His guidance to the pioneering minority was confirmed by the words from the enemy, "Come up to us."

Jonathan spoke in bold authority to his partner, an authority that came out of his humility and assurance that they were in God's will—plus a total dependence on God. "Come up after me, for the LORD has delivered them into the hand of Israel" (verse 12).

Conversely, the Philistines manifested a spirit of arrogance and self-dependence—both rooted in pride. *Pride comes before a fall.* (See Proverbs 16:18.) Notice that they had said, "Come up to us, and *we* will show *you* something."

Jonathan and his armorbearer still had to climb steep precipices and engage in fierce battle. An astonishing display of God's miraculous power followed a remarkable display of unity in teamwork: "And Jonathan climbed up on his hands and knees with his armorbearer after him; and they fell before Jonathan. And as he came after him, his armorbearer killed them" (verse 13).

It takes more humility to function effectively in teamwork than to do great exploits alone. That is one of the reasons for this significant victory. "The first slaughter which Jonathan and his armorbearer made was about twenty men within about half an acre of land" (verse 14). Two men and God overpowered twenty men in half an acre of land!

In Psalm 18 David recounts exactly the same supernatural takeovers when he was being hounded like an animal:

> With your help I can advance against a troop; with my God I can scale a wall. . . . He makes my feet like the feet of a deer; he causes me to stand on the heights. . . . You provide a broad path for my feet, so that my ankles do not give way. . . . I pursued my enemies and overtook them; I did not turn back till they were destroyed. I crushed them so that they could not rise; they fell beneath my feet. You armed me with strength for battle; you humbled my adversaries before me.
>
> Verses 29, 33, 36–39 NIV

Back to Jonathan. Look at the results of this military phenomenon: "And there was trembling in the camp, in the field, and among all the people. The garrison and the raiders also trembled; and the earth quaked, so that it was a very great trembling" (1 Samuel 14:15). God's explosive power broke out on all the people, with trembling—everybody was affected drastically, including the earth, which was quaking, under a very great trembling. There was great terror everywhere, and look how the Philistines are described: "There was the multitude, melting away; and they went here and there. . . . The noise which was in the camp of the Philistines continued to increase. . . . There was very great confusion" (verses 16, 19–20). Fear took over as the Philistines began to fight each other, "and indeed every man's sword was against his neighbor" (verse 20).

Wow, what a mind-boggling takeover from headquarters heaven! In addition, the Israelites who lived among the Philistines as slaves revolted and joined in the battle against their masters. Another group did the same. We read in verse 22, "Likewise all the men of Israel who had hidden in the mountains of Ephraim, when they heard that the Philistines fled, they also followed hard after them in battle."

What had started out as two young men plus God, risking their lives to defeat the enemy, ended up as a massive victory for the whole nation. All heaven broke loose, and God got *all the glory*! "So *the* LORD *saved Israel* that day" (verse 23, emphasis added).

Here is the summary of the success of these two young men:

- Their dependence was entirely upon God.
- They were determined that all the glory would go to God.
- They manifested biblical unity based on genuine humility.
- They diligently sought God for His directions and totally obeyed Him.

After a victory, our biggest opposition often comes from jealousy in other leaders. Because of jealousy after David slew Goliath, Saul tried many times to kill David. Now, Saul manifests jealousy toward Jonathan and tries to have him killed. Older leaders very much need to guard their hearts against this horrible sin of jealousy—especially toward younger leaders whom God uses in different and possibly more powerful ways than God has used them. "Jealousy is cruel as the grave; its flashes are flashes of fire, a most vehement flame" (Song of Solomon 8:6

RSV). "Wrath is cruel, anger is overwhelming; but who can stand before jealousy?" (Proverbs 27:4 RSV).

Jonathan nearly lost his life after the battle due to a foolish rule Saul imposed on the people. Not knowing about the rule, Jonathan innocently broke it. Saul pronounced his death. (See 1 Samuel 14:24–45.) But I love how God intervened on Jonathan's behalf through the people. After Saul had pronounced his son's death sentence, the people recognized that Jonathan and his armorbearer had paid an enormous price for victory, and that they had done it in obedience to God's directions. The people's words were, "As the LORD lives, not one hair of [Jonathan's] head shall fall to the ground, for he has worked with God this day" (verse 45).

This proves *again* that no man or devil can thwart the will of God for our lives. If we will pay the high price of being the pioneering minority plus God, a whole nation can be brought out of darkness into the light and brought into freedom from satanic forces.

In order to effectively apply everything I have written today, we have to be thoroughly convinced of the following truths from God's Word. They involve God's *position, power, purposes, plans* and *perspectives* related to the unreached nations. Let's focus more closely on each of these. Our *faith* is according to our *focus*.

God's Position

God's position refers to His supreme authority and sovereign control over the nations:

> How awesome is the LORD Most High, the great King over all the earth! . . . God reigns over the nations; God is seated on his holy throne.
>
> Psalm 47:2, 8 NIV1984

112

All the ends of the earth will remember and turn to the LORD,
and all the families of the nations will bow down before him,
for dominion belongs to the LORD and He rules over the nations.

Psalm 22:27–28 NIV1984

God's Power

God's power over the nations is shown in these verses:

The LORD will lay bare His holy arm in the sight of all the
nations, and all the ends of the earth will see the salvation of
our God.

Isaiah 52:10 NIV1984

Be strong and courageous; do not be afraid nor dismayed . . .
before all the multitude. . . . With [them] is an arm of flesh; but
with us is the LORD our God, to help us and to fight our battles.

2 Chronicles 32:7–8

Here is an illustration: About 23 years ago, a young Christian
couple were called of God to go to Uganda as missionaries.
The husband, Gary Skinner, was from South Africa, and his
wife, Marilyn, was from Canada. They had only been there
four months when one night 25 men came knocking at their
door. Marilyn was alone in the house with her young children.

"Open up!" the men demanded. They intended to rob, rape
and possibly even kill Marilyn. She and the children hid under the
bed. The men kept knocking. Marilyn kept quoting the Scripture
God had given her that very day: "No weapon formed against you
shall prosper" (Isaiah 54:17). Unable to get through the wooden
door after three hours of banging, the men finally left.

On another occasion, three men did break in and rob the
house. Tying Gary and Marilyn up with electric cords, they put
a gun to Gary's head and demanded more money.

"We don't have any more, so you may as well shoot us," Marilyn responded.

The man pulled the trigger, but the gun did not fire. He tried several more times. It still did not go off.

"Are you Christians?" the men asked. When Marilyn affirmed yes, the men fled.

The Skinners stayed at their post and today have a church of twenty thousand. In a country that for years suffered under Idi Amin's corrupt rule, where AIDS has decimated the population and marauding bands of boy soldiers have invaded, a change is happening. Uganda is now being invaded by the culture of Jesus.

If God can do this in Uganda, He can do it in any part of the world. Let's pray that God will raise up those who have the courage to fulfill the conditions.

God's Purposes and Plans

God's purposes and plans related to the nations are shown in these verses:

> And they sang a new song, saying: "You are worthy to take the scroll and to open its seals, because you were slain, and with your blood you purchased for God persons from every tribe and language and people and nation."
>
> Revelation 5:9 NIV

> "Ask me, and I will make the nations your inheritance, the ends of the earth your possession."
>
> Psalm 2:8 NIV

> "Surely you will summon nations you know not, and nations that do not know you will hasten to you, because of the LORD your God, the Holy One of Israel, for he has endowed you with splendor."
>
> Isaiah 55:5 NIV1984

Here is another illustration: A group of Otomi believers in the village of San Nicholas in the Mezquital Valley of Mexico had left the religious traditions of the Otomis and had become Christians. They faced increasing persecution, which led to the other villagers demanding that they leave. The believers settled on a bare hill on the other side of the Ixmiquilpan, a place where no one else wanted to live.

One day, the Christians heard about a plan that was to be carried out that same night to exterminate them all. One of the women believers who had been there the longest went to every hut, urging the people to pray for help and put their trust in God. She said, "Don't be afraid. God isn't dead!"

Some were afraid to come into the open on top of the hill for fear of bullets from an ambush. But gradually, the trembling believers slowly assembled. In simple faith they pled for God's protection and for Him to somehow display His glory. In faith they went back to their huts and slept.

The next day, in the streets of Ixmiquilpan, people gathered in small groups, staring at the Christians and whispering among themselves. Gradually the story became known. Several hundred men, intent on exterminating every Christian and armed with dynamite and other weapons, had gathered the night before at the bottom of the hill. At a given signal, they started up toward the believers, when suddenly God turned on the fire of His power. To their horror, they saw the whole hilltop was covered with a glaringly bright light, with the little church building in full view. They could see soldiers circling the hilltop, all holding guns and all ready to fire. Trumpets began playing loudly.

The angry mob reported the next day that they could not get up the hill because they could not pass the "guards." Every Christian was spared from death. They knew that our miracle-working God had spotted them when He was looking

115

for someone to whom He could display His glory by the fire of His power at a time of desperate need. They proved that powerful promise in Psalm 34:7: "The angel of the LORD encamps around all those who fear Him, and [He] delivers them."

At one point it had seemed that the little Otomi congregation might be snuffed out in a single night. But now there are some 5,000 believers scattered in 54 village congregations, and they have the New Testament translated and printed in their own Otomi language through Wycliffe Bible Translators. Because all heaven had been loosed!

Jesus said, "I will build my church, and the gates of hell shall not prevail against it" (Matthew 16:18 ESV). We must only and always be impressed with the One who said these words—never the one who challenges them.

God's Perspective

God's perspective of the enemy, satanic forces, must become our perspective:

> For this purpose the Son of God was manifested, that He might destroy the works of the devil.
>
> 1 John 3:8 NIV

When Jesus said on the cross, "It is finished," all satanic activities on earth became illegal. "And having disarmed the powers and authorities, he made a public spectacle of them, triumphing over them by the cross" (Colossians 2:15 NIV). Satan is nothing but a fallen angel doomed to eternal destruction. We must never be impressed with that status!

We must never ever think that it is hard for God to reach the Muslims, atheists, communists, Buddhists, Shintoists, Hindus, humanists and nothing-ists. It is only difficult for Christians who limit God through unbelief. When we give God fervent praise for who He is, He will rise up and display His power. "The LORD will march out like a champion, like a warrior he will stir up his zeal; with a shout he will raise the battle cry and will triumph over his enemies" (Isaiah 42:13).

- Light is more powerful than darkness.
- Truth is stronger than error.
- There is more grace in God's heart than sin in human hearts.
- There is more power in the Holy Spirit to convict human hearts of sin than in the power of satanic forces to tempt them to sin.
- There is more power in one drop of the shed blood of the Lord Jesus to cleanse human hearts from the stain of sin, than in the accumulated filth of people's sin from Adam and Eve until now.

Hallelujah! Our God reigns!

In order to live in Trinity unity, we can find ourselves in sticky and tricky circumstances. The next chapter will help us navigate them.

10

Maintaining Unity in Difficult Circumstances

What do we do when we see something in another Christian that we know is wrong? I have a simple little saying to help me in these situations: "Don't say it—pray it."

In 1 Peter 4:8 we read, "And above all things have fervent love for one another, for 'love will cover a multitude of sins.'"

We "cover" the person's wrongdoing by not talking to anyone about it, but by asking God in love and faith to reveal it to him or her in His way and time. God is good at doing that—to us all.

Before we pass on any negative comment about anyone, we should bear in mind what God says about doing that:

Brothers, do not slander one another. Anyone who speaks against his brother or judges him, speaks against the law and judges it. When you judge the law, you are not keeping it, but sitting in judgment on it. There is only one Lawgiver and Judge, the one

who is able to save and to destroy. But you—who are you to
judge your neighbor?

James 4:11–12 NIV1984

Jesus commands us in Matthew 7:1–2 (ESV), "Judge not, that
you be not judged. For with the judgment you pronounce you
will be judged." Think about it! We come under God's judgment
every time we speak negatively about others.

In many years of counseling people going through difficult
and perplexing circumstances, there have been times when the
Holy Spirit has prompted me to ask the question, "Have there
been times in your life when you have judged others in similar
circumstances?" Invariably, after some thought, the answer has
come back yes. Mercifully, after confession and repentance, a
turnaround has come in their circumstances in time.

If the person concerned persists in the wrongdoing and we
have earned the right to speak to him or her because of our
level of friendship, then we seek God about whether to speak
up. If God answers yes, then we make sure such conversations
are always done in love and take place privately.

Matthew 18:15 says, "If your brother sins against you, go
and tell him his fault between you and him alone." Ephesians 4:15 talks about "speaking the truth in love." Disobedi-
ence to either of these commands will produce unnecessary
pain to the hearer.

If we are in a position of leadership, it is essential to get the
facts first—not hearsay. It is equally important that we give equal
listening time to both parties in a dispute. I once failed to do
this, to my deep regret, but I greatly learned from it. "The first
one to plead his cause seems right, until his neighbor comes
and examines him" (Proverbs 18:17).

Leaders should also be praying for revelation of what is truth
in a situation, for prepared hearts to receive the truth, for God's
mercy to be released and for unity to be the outcome. "These

120

are the things you shall do: Speak each man the truth to his neighbor; give judgment in your gates for truth, justice, and peace" (Zechariah 8:16).

The Bible also says, "As a man thinketh in his heart, so is he" (Proverbs 23:7 KJV). So our thoughts sound as loud in heaven as our words do on earth. That is worth pondering! That is why God says in Zechariah 8:17, "'Let none of you think evil in your heart against your neighbor . . . for all these are things that I hate,' says the LORD."

What do we do when we hear a negative comment about someone we know who has a proven righteous character? If the comment does not match up, throw it out, forget it and vindicate the person. In Isaiah 54:17 God says that He vindicates the righteous. He uses people to do that—you and me.

What do we do when we hear a negative comment about someone, and we have heard only good about the person before, yet we do not know their character? I am going to keep believing the good about the person until God should choose to convince me otherwise. This puts the responsibility on God to make the next move, should there be need for change.

What if we will be in a group situation with that person? Ask God to reveal whether the person is innocent or guilty. He is the only One who knows the up-to-date condition of the human heart. (See 2 Chronicles 6:30.) If God reveals to you that the person is innocent, vindicate him or her. If guilty, then pray that God will reveal that to leadership and that it will be brought to light. If we are the leadership, we must deal with the situation, as I have already stated. If we do not deal with it, two things will eventuate:

1. God will hold us accountable. "Take heed to yourselves. If your brother sins against you, rebuke him; and if he repents, forgive him" (Luke 17:3).
2. The enemy (Satan) will be able to attack a whole group on that particular sin.

Paul addresses the need to deal with the sin of immorality in the whole of chapter 5 in his first epistle to the Corinthians, and how this sin defiles the Church. Also, Paul exhorts Timothy to take a strong stand in openly correcting leaders who resist biblical ways of bringing correction:

> Do not entertain an accusation against an elder unless it is brought by two or three witnesses. But those elders who are sinning you are to reprove before everyone, so that the others may take warning.
>
> 1 Timothy 5:19–20 NIV

Twice in my lifetime I have witnessed this passage being carried out. In each church, only those in membership were present. On each occasion, exactly what the Word of God said would happen, did! The fear of the Lord was strongly evident.

In 2 Timothy 4:1–2 (NIV) Paul encourages Timothy to take seriously his leadership responsibilities, knowing that it is the only way of maintaining biblical unity:

> In the presence of God and of Christ Jesus, who will judge the living and the dead, and in view of his appearing and his kingdom, I give you this charge: Preach the word; be prepared in season and out of season; correct, rebuke and encourage—with great patience and careful instruction.

God has an equally clear warning in His Word about the danger of speaking critically of spiritual leaders whom God is using: "Do not touch My anointed ones, and do My prophets no harm" (Psalm 105:15). I have a whole chapter on this subject in my book *Intimate Friendship with God* (Chosen, 2008). I share how God dealt with me severely about this when I was a younger woman. It forever changed my life.

I also remember how it deeply impacted Jim and me when a pastor friend of ours told us the following story just before he retired from the ministry. It took place during the time when he was a young minister doing everything he knew of to be obedient to God's direction. Every time he would bring the word of the Lord to the people in his church and then encourage them to act on it, three older men would oppose him. This happened consistently, and all he knew to do was to put them in God's hands, believing He would deal with them somehow, some way.

God did! Within six months, our pastor friend had conducted each of the three men's funeral services. The pastor told us he had never before told anyone that story.

We had better take God seriously when we are hindering unity through criticizing God's anointed servant leaders. Think about what happened to Korah, Dathan and Abiram when they accused Moses and Aaron of exalting themselves above the assembly of the Lord, killing the people in the wilderness and lording it over them (See Numbers 16:3, 13). "The ground split apart under them, and the earth opened its mouth and swallowed them up, with their households and all the men with Korah, with all their goods" (Numbers 16:31–32).

What about pausing right now and asking the Holy Spirit to bring to your remembrance anyone you have criticized, specifically spiritual leaders whom God is using? We do ourselves a favor by confessing and repenting of this hindrance to unity. Restitution is part of repentance. We go back to the person to whom we spoke the criticism and acknowledge our sin. Forgiveness from God is then released, and we are wiser. "When pride comes, then comes shame; but with the humble is wisdom" (Proverbs 11:2).

Let's defeat the devil's tactics to divide us. Let's become peacemakers and unifiers. Let's follow Psalm 34:14—"Depart from evil and do good; seek peace and pursue it"—as a way of life.

What do we do when we have to bring correction to others? I find great enjoyment and fulfillment in bringing encouragement to others. The Holy Spirit has made it part of my DNA. I have therefore needed every Scripture I could find that encourages me when God requires me to bring correction to others in difficult circumstances. Here are two of them: "He who rebukes a man will find more favor afterward than he who flatters with the tongue" (Proverbs 28:23). Notice the word *afterward*—not straightaway. And "Rebuke a wise man and he will love you. Instruct a wise man and he will be wiser still; teach a righteous man and he will add to his learning" (Proverbs 9:8–9 NIV 1984).

Now, let's take encouragement from what the Bible says about when we must be corrected by others. If it is the truth spoken in love, privately, at the right time, we should receive it with gratitude because we will learn from it. "A fool despises his father's instruction, but he who receives correction is prudent" (Proverbs 15:5). "Let the righteous strike me; it shall be a kindness. And let him rebuke me; it shall be as excellent oil; let my head not refuse it" (Psalm 141:5).

If Abigail had not acted quickly and gone to speak to David in gentleness, humility and wisdom—which included a rebuke and a warning—many lives would have been lost and David would have come under God's judgment. If David had not had the humility of heart to receive this input from a godly woman, he would never have had her later as his wife and the mother of one of his children.

Much destiny hinges upon whether or not we choose to exercise the humility that produces biblical unity, especially in difficult circumstances.

I salute everyone who has come this far with me in pursuit of Trinity unity. In the next chapter, we will check ourselves out to see how far that is. It can only encourage us or further enlighten us, so again, stay for the ride!

11

Characteristics of Those Committed to Trinity Unity

Let's have an honesty session and evaluate our lives using the standard of God's Word on the subject of Trinity unity.

The first characteristic of those committed to Trinity unity is that we have a genuine spirit of humility that makes it easy for us to honor one another. We understand Romans 12:10 (RSV), "Love one another with brotherly affection; outdo one another in showing honor." Or as another version says, "Take delight in honoring each other" (ESV). We are the first to honor and encourage spiritual leaders, as we are exhorted to do in 1 Timothy 5:17 (RSV), "Let the elders who rule well be considered worthy of double honor, especially those who labor in preaching and teaching."

There is a high price to pay to live up to God's standard for a preacher and Bible teacher. The basics are found in Ezra 7:10, "For Ezra had prepared his heart to seek the law of the LORD, and to do it, and to teach statutes and ordinances in Israel."

The order is important. First, Ezra took his ministry very seriously. He made sure he had a clean heart—no undealt-with sin toward God or men.

Second, he searched the Scriptures to find out what God had to say about the subject on which God had first directed him to speak.

Third, he made sure he was living those truths as a way of life.

Fourth, only then did Ezra teach those truths to others.

These are the "tip of the iceberg" points from one of the many important messages God has given me for spiritual leaders, a message titled "The Price to Preach."

The second characteristic is that we are convinced no one person, or any group of persons, has all the truth. We see the need, therefore, to listen and learn from *all* other believers and encourage others to do the same.

It has never ceased to amaze me how so many denominations really believe they have the edge on all the truth. Oh, really? I am convinced that God has graced a broad spectrum of the Body of Christ with differing emphases of the truths from His Word, *so that* we would have the humility to see our desperate need to listen and to learn from each other.

It is exciting to learn. Only God can tolerate the boredom of listening to the same old same old. I guess that is because He has never ceased creating, because creativity is part of who He is; He creates in ways we humans cannot see or would not believe even if He told us! Food for thought.

The point is, true humility of heart will inevitably be on the alert to listen and to learn about spiritual truths from anyone or by any means God puts across our paths. That produces really exciting results—in literature, media, science and in many other ways.

Since writing these words, I watched a reputable Christian TV program where the TV host was interviewing a deeply committed Christian doctor from Africa. The doctor had a Ph.D. in matters related to the brain and was specializing in helping people come to wholeness through "brain mapping." The program was highly informative and fascinating, to say the least. Best of all, the technique is producing wonderful results and God is being glorified.

The part of this doctor's story that impressed me particularly was that as a young boy of six, brought up in a godly home with fine Christian parents, this doctor had a series of dreams where he saw himself working among white people, doing exactly what he is doing today. At that time it seemed impossible, and even today his family members in Africa find it hard to believe.

Oh, the wonder of the increased knowledge that God is sovereignly releasing in the earth today to help bring wholeness to mind, body, soul and spirit. This fulfills Daniel 12:4, "knowledge shall increase," and Colossians 1:28–29, "Him we preach, warning every man and teaching every man in all wisdom. . . ."

We should never close our minds to something because we have not heard of it before, or because we cannot understand it. Neither should we be gullible about every new thing that comes across our radar. The more we live in the fear of the Lord, which the Bible says is both the beginning of wisdom and instruction in wisdom, the more we will be given the wisdom to discern the true from the false—in everything.

The third characteristic of those committed to Trinity unity is that we have no reserves about worshiping and fellowshiping with *all* of God's children. Paul could write to the believers at Ephesus and Colossae and say, "Since we have heard of your faith in Christ Jesus and of your love for *all* the saints."

We will only be as comfortable in heaven as we are comfortable in associating with *all* of God's children on earth. What will that scenario look like? Let's take a look at a limited cross section just for starters: Roman Catholics, Seventh Day Adventists, Pentecostals, charismatics, Lutherans, Anglicans, Mexicans, American Indians and Asians. Or the host people of any of the other nations and people groups like the Maoris of New Zealand, the Samoans and Fijians in the South Pacific, or the Eskimos or the Aboriginals in Australia.

Some of all of the above will be there, and could well be honored by the Lord Jesus way ahead of us. I have had the immense joy of ministering to and with all but the last one on that list—and that is only because I have not had the chance with that group.

Jesus, when on earth, honored a Gentile soldier for his faith in a Jewish setting, and He honored an obscure, poor widow for her giving. He frequently told His adult audiences to become like the little children.

Let's ask the Holy Spirit to give us Jesus' perspective on all things. If we are serious and have faith, He will. It means asking for the mind of Christ, as described in Philippians 2.

Paul evidently took special delight in the Thessalonian believers. He wrote, "We are bound to thank God always for you, brethren . . . because your faith grows exceedingly, and the love of every one of you all abounds toward each other, so that we ourselves boast of you among the churches of God" (2 Thessalonians 1:3–4). This is just one example of how special they were to him—he even bragged about them to other churches. Why? They were increasing in humility and love toward each other. That is where it is at!

The "spiritually natural" outworking of this level of loving everyone is that we will welcome the prospect of working alongside other Christians in teamwork, another characteristic of Trinity unity. We will do this regardless of differing viewpoints or interpretations of Scripture, and coming from the conviction that we are open to learning from others.

In Galatians 5:13 (RSV) Paul tells us, "Through love be servants of one another." A servant listens and learns. He does not dictate how he should serve another or tell the other what his need is, but asks, "What are your needs? How may I serve you in ways that would please you?"

Paul gives us more powerful concepts about how humility works in teamwork in Ephesians 4:1–3 (RSV):

> I therefore, a prisoner for the Lord, beg you to lead a life worthy of the calling to which you have been called, with all lowliness and meekness, with patience, forbearing one another in love, eager to maintain the unity of the Spirit in the bond of peace.

When we really start living that standard of biblical unity, this next characteristic should flow out of us as a way of life—we will delight in expressing encouragement and gratitude to any other believer God is using to extend His Kingdom.

Paul saw that his beloved Thessalonians were doing this, so he affirmed them: "Therefore encourage one another and build one another up, just as you are doing" (1 Thessalonians 5:11, RSV). In other words, "Well done, guys. I've noticed how well you relate to one another. Keep it up."

Paul also knew that if we do not live this way in teamwork, we will need to ask the Holy Spirit to show us if the root cause is insecurity in us, or jealousy. "Let us have no self conceit, no provoking of one another, no envy of one another" (Galatians 5:26, RSV). We need to confess and repent of those root sins before we will be released to be encouragers and people who express their need of others. (See Proverbs 28:13.)

The next characteristic of Bible unity has two parts. I have already shared them, but I am repeating them so that this chapter can stand alone as a checkup.

A. We will love to promote appreciation of one person to another. Paul wanted the Roman believers to make this a way of life when he wrote to them, "Let us then pursue what makes for peace and for mutual upbuilding" (Romans 14:19, RSV). Many years ago I inquired of the Holy Spirit how I could do this in some practical way. The answer came back, spoken into my spirit. It is part B of this characteristic:

B. "When you hear a negative comment about a person, never pass it on to the person to whom it was directed." I saw that this fitted with Psalm 34:14, "Seek peace and pursue it," and with Matthew 5:9, "Blessed are the peacemakers. . . ."

Another characteristic is that we see our need to receive from others. In Trinity unity love, we feel a great need for the love, encouragement and prayers of others. If the apostle Paul could express his need, especially for prayer support, how much more should we? In 2 Corinthians 1:11 (RSV) he says, "You also must help us by prayer, so that many will give thanks on our behalf for the blessing granted us in answer to many prayers."

In Colossians 4:3–4 Paul calls again from prison for prayer support, mentioning his chains. And in verse 18 he writes, "Remember my chains." He knew it took a lot of grace to cope with the debilitating effect of trying to function daily, let alone write, with those heavy metals chafing his wrists.

How grateful we should be that Paul endured the inevitable pain, humiliation and suffering—mentally, emotionally and physically—of being chained to a Roman soldier in a Roman prison, to give us those wonderful epistles. I am deeply impacted by the Holy Spirit as I write these words. I have often asked the Lord to tell Paul in heaven how much I love and appreciate him. How I long for Paul to know that he is being honored.

All of us need to give and receive genuine expressions of love and encouragement as a way of life in this pleasurable unity.

This glorifies God. What about stopping right now and asking the Holy Spirit to bring to your mind someone who needs a loving, encouraging word from you? It does not need to be lengthy. An appropriate card . . . or a note . . . or a phone call . . . or an email . . . or face-to-face at church will do it.

Recently I was talking to a serious-minded young worship leader of a vital church I was visiting. I said, "Today the worship seemed to be at a deeper, penetrating level—though I had not thought it previously shallow. Can you explain?"

To my great surprise, he shared with unusual intensity how God had totally worked over his whole spiritual life during a twelve-month period while he was slowly reading and applying my book *The Fire of God* (Destiny Image, 2008). "Everything in me is radically changed," he said. "The new songs we sang in worship today have come as a result."

While I received enormous encouragement from him, which I needed, I pressed another question: "Is there any more unity among your team of singers and instrumentalists than you had before?"

His answer surprised me again. "Absolutely. We had hardly any, in that we never really knew each other at all. Now I care about each one and have pursued a genuine relationship with each team member. We are now in wonderful unity as a real team."

> May the God of steadfastness and encouragement grant you to live in such harmony with one another, in accord with Christ Jesus, that together you may with one voice glorify the God and Father of our Lord Jesus Christ.
>
> Romans 15:5–6 RSV

Another characteristic is that we also realize our great need of God-given friendships that lovingly bring correction to us when needed. "Let a good man strike or rebuke me in kindness"

(Psalm 141:5 RSV). If we fail to exercise the humility of receiving a loving rebuke, we will fail to receive the wisdom God wanted to give us for future occasions. We do ourselves a favor by living this standard of biblical unity. "He who disdains instruction despises his own soul, but he who heeds rebuke gets understanding" (Proverbs 15:32).

Still another characteristic of those committed to living in Trinity unity is that we take pleasure in submitting to God's order related to authority, through leaders and the ministry giftings outlined in God's Word. "Remember your leaders, those who spoke to you the Word of God, consider the outcome of their life, and imitate their faith" (Hebrews 13:7 RSV).

Mavericks (loners) do not fit well with these truths. People manifesting an independent spirit will not be happy with them either!

If the spiritual leaders who are over us in authority are living the characteristics of this biblical unity, it will be easy to submit to them. If not, we need to submit to them anyway and leave the outcome to God, who will be testing us. Or we need to seek God about whether, in His timing, He could be redirecting us. If so, we should always leave somewhere with a noncritical, Christlike attitude.

We will do ourselves the greatest favor by carefully reading and applying the challenging but far-reaching effects of the truths in the final chapter. This is where the rubber meets the road, and it is red hot with divine purpose for you and for me!

12

The Dynamics of Togetherness to Reach Our Cities for God

The humility of togetherness is beautifully illustrated in 2 Chronicles 3:11, where we read that the wings of the cherubim placed in the Holy Place in Solomon's Temple touched each other. Also, in Ezekiel 1:9–12 (RSV) the wings of the living creatures touched one another: "They went every one straight forward, without turning as they went. . . . Each creature had two wings, each of which touched the wing of another . . . and each went straight forward; wherever the spirit would go, they went."

There was absolutely no way they could be independent of each other because their wing tips had to touch each other. As a result, they made maximum progress, under the Holy Spirit's direction. We will discern the Holy Spirit's direction and make far more progress when we learn to see our desperate need of being in touch with one another. Let's go out of our way to spend time with people we are not used to having time with, expecting to enjoy them and learn from them. Let's go beyond tolerating or accepting each other and have some "wing touching" with each other. That means closer unity coming from a closer togetherness through fellowshiping together, having meals together, praying together and worshiping God together.

While I was pondering the truths that I have shared, in silence before the Lord, the following stanza came to my mind:

> The roots of unity are humility.
> The fruits of humility are love.
> There's still room for our diversity.
> But the world will say, "It's from above."

Biblical Togetherness

Let's look now at the ways the humility of biblical togetherness needs to express itself in the Body of Christ in our cities.

One way is seeing our need to pray together regularly across denominational and racial lines. The Word of God gives the blueprint. We cannot improve on it. Before there was the big breakthrough in evangelism in the city of Jerusalem, the early Church believers were together in one place, in one accord, with one purpose—to pray together. Acts 1:14 (NIV) says, "They all joined together constantly in prayer, along with the women and Mary the Mother of Jesus, and with His brothers." There were about 120 people, and "When the day of Pentecost came they were all together in one place" (Acts 2:1 NIV). We must start there and keep going back there until God breaks through. That group had not always been in unity. Previously, according to John 7:5, Jesus' brothers had not believed in Him: "For even His brothers did not believe in Him."

We also need to come together as congregations to worship and to learn from God's Word together. We need to invite other churches to come to our church so that we can "in honor prefer them." We need to ask other pastors to speak. We need to invite other church choirs to minister. We need to make sure we have a mixture of ethnic and racial groups, as well as denominations, wherever possible.

God has plans for every one of us to be involved with other ethnic groups and other denominations, other cultures and other age groups, among Christians and non-Christians, for a far broader base of unity, so that the lost may be evangelized.

To broaden our unity bases, we have to make racial changes and get out of our comfort zones in relation to those with whom we fellowship and minister. Pastor Jack Hayford was an outstanding example of bringing unity among all peoples, period, when he pastored The Church On The Way for over thirty years. And he still is an example.

To bring the early Church to the next plateau, God took two vital men—known to God but unknown to each other, living in different cities—and linked them together in fellowship and ministry functions. They represented two totally different races of people. God wanted to break down racial prejudices and remove the high wall of religious differences between them. Peter at that time was the undisputed leader of the church in Jerusalem, having been greatly used of God to evangelize the Jews. He had baptized thousands and had been mightily used of God in the miraculous. He was a dynamic spiritual leader, but like so many today, he had a huge missing dimension to his ministry. God was about to correct it.

God gave Peter a vision of different kinds of animals, reptiles and birds together inside a sheet and told him to eat them all—it was okay; they were all clean. Then He told Peter to go without any hesitation with the men who had just arrived at the door, as they had been sent by Him.

The implications for Peter were enormous. He had to change his whole concept of what was right and wrong in relation to the people to whom he was to go. It was against the law for a Jew to associate with or visit a foreigner. (See Acts 10:28.) It meant radical changes of mind and lifestyle, as Jews and Gentiles never ate together. To the Jews, the Gentiles ate unclean foods; therefore, there was no social interaction. When God showed Peter there was now no distinction of meals, He also revealed that from now on, Jews and Gentiles were to fellowship and eat together on equal terms. In Acts 10 and 11, Peter had to get up and leave the securities of the known, and go to the unknown for his next ministry assignment.

Look at the lessons we can learn from the lives of the other key people God used to bring the early Church to a new plateau. Cornelius was a Roman military captain in the city of Caesarea. Acts 10:2 says he was "a devout man who feared God with all his household" (RSV). He was one of the class of Gentiles who gave general adherence to the Jewish faith, worship and practice without submitting to circumcision and becoming a full proselyte. He was involved with meeting the needs of the poor and needy, made prayer to God a way of life and was a man of high reputation within the whole Jewish nation. (See Acts 10:22.)

Obviously impressed with Cornelius' life, God dispatched an angel to him with a message saying, "Your prayers and gifts to the poor have come up as a memorial offering before God" (Acts 10:4 NIV). Think about it—he was a God-fearing man of prayer and fasting who had never heard the Gospel. Interesting thought.

I believe Cornelius' prayers had a lot to do with God's plans for him to become the first Gentile Christian. He was obviously living up to the light he knew and was influencing others to do the same. For example, when the angel told him to send men to Joppa to get Peter, Cornelius assigned a God-fearing soldier close to him to head up the team.

Cornelius' response to the news that this man, Peter, was coming with a message that would bring salvation to him and his household (see Acts 11:14) was unquestioning, unconditional obedience—the only thing that impresses God!

Think of the implications to Cornelius. Being an uncircumcised Gentile, he would face the possibility of rejection from Simon Peter, a Jew. Would Peter believe him and receive his messengers?

Cornelius was a man of faith. The angel said it; he believed it. He did not try to rationalize, like Zechariah in Luke 1:18 when the angel Gabriel announced that his wife would have a baby boy. He did not argue with God, like Moses at his ordination at the burning bush. Cornelius feared God, not man. He obeyed. In faith, he called together his relatives and close friends and had his house full, with many people assembled. (See Acts 10:27.) He manifested great humility and gratitude toward Peter. Then he said, in effect, "We're all here before God now, ready to hear everything the Lord has ordered you to say" (see Acts 10:33). (Those words are the ultimate introduction to a preacher and teacher of God's Word.)

We need to ask God who our Corneliuses are. Who are the people with whom we would not normally link for ministry purposes and fellowship? I believe God is speaking to us through this chapter in Acts 10, telling us that He wants to bring the Body of Christ worldwide to a whole new plateau of divine purpose in relation to unity, which will result in an explosion of successful evangelism of unprecedented proportions.

The world needs to see us together denominationally and racially in order for John 17:23 to become a reality through our working together to serve the community. This needs to be both in ordinary times of general need and in times of crisis. This is demonstrated by the following account:

In Washington, D.C., Dr. Louis Evans Jr., the former pastor of the National Presbyterian Church of Washington, D.C., linked together with the late Dr. Sam Hines, a Jamaican pastor who had a church in the poor part of town, where they fed the poor five days a week. Their people went out in pairs, one from each of the churches just mentioned, going door-to-door and asking people if they needed practical help related to their homes, and then providing that help. Wow, was that ever a great success for the extension of God's Kingdom! Unity and servanthood. Humility and love. Unbeatable combinations.

We also need to be evangelizing together. This can be done by bringing in an anointed evangelist, with a proven character of integrity, at the direction of the Lord's leading. God has His servants who fit these criteria and should be used to the maximum. One of the most effective ways of uniting the Body of Christ, maturing the Christian, and evangelizing and discipling the lost is through this proven method. Billy and Franklin Graham's crusades have been and are a primary example.

What is happening in the city of Sanford, Florida, as I write is an excellent example of the Trinity unity this book is all about. I love the passionate way that Steve Strang has written about events there, and he is also in the process of making a documentary film that shows what happened. It started with the tragic shooting death of seventeen-year-old Trayvon Martin, allegedly the result of racial profiling. Several different ethnic groups got involved in the saga, and the media jumped on the inflammatory side, playing up the negatives—reporting on the hateful rhetoric in use and the rallies and protests held nationwide that produced unrest and confusion.

But the leadership in the Body of Christ has jumped in head-first and feetfirst to counterattack it all with a magnificent display of Trinity unity, according to Strang's report. A cross section of denominations and races stood shoulder-to-shoulder (you could not see daylight between them), displaying the glory Jesus spoke of in John 17 that would be upon those who would live out the principles of humility, love and unity. These united pastors and believers continue to work toward forgiveness, healing and reconciliation both in Sanford and around the country.

We need to pray for Holy Spirit revelation and conviction of the pride and prejudice that still exists in the Body of Christ worldwide between the races and ethnic groups, between males and females, between denominations, between parachurches and independent churches.

On Daystar Television Network, Jim and I recently watched an extremely powerful night of historic significance for the nation of America. James Robison and a unique cross section of other like-minded, strong spiritual leaders spoke with authority and passion to an audience of seven thousand people who had gathered in a large church in Dallas, Texas, under the theme "Under God Indivisible." It all related to our desperate need to stand up, speak out and be involved in every way that we can in helping to stem the tide of the minority in America who are trying to rob us of the very foundational Judeo-Christian rights of faith, freedom and family. The call was to unite God's people at any cost for this God-ordained cause at this critical hour in this nation.

Each participant was an absolute winner. I responded to what each said with thunderous amens. That night of strong unity and powerful truth, spoken in genuine love, would put a big smile on God's face and remind the devil that Jesus said, "I will build my church, and the gates of hell shall not prevail against it" (Matthew 16:18 ESV).

We have learned that biblical unity is rooted in humility. Humility manifests itself in loving togetherness. Biblical togetherness says, "I need you, to learn from you." The early Church was characterized by this kind of togetherness. It was a major reason for their explosive impact upon the then-known world. They knew and believed that *united we win*, and that when we are united, all heaven will break loose.

They prayed together, were empowered by the Holy Spirit together, preached together, evangelized together, taught the Word of God together, assembled themselves together, talked together, shared their possessions together, worshiped together, rejoiced together, sang together, suffered and were persecuted together, comforted themselves together, took communion together, shared experiences together, wept together and lived together. Each of those statements has a Bible reference.

As Christians committed to the Lordship of Jesus Christ, we know that when He comes again we are all going up together, and we will spend eternity together. So if we do not want to be uncomfortable in heaven, we had better experience the humility of true togetherness down here.

I invite you, dear reader, to pray the following prayer. If you sincerely pray this prayer in faith, God will surely answer it and use you in powerful ways as a unifier.

Prayer of Commitment to Live in Trinity Unity

Dear God, I believe that Trinity unity is possible. I want to experience it with every other child of God. Right now I ask for it, and by faith I receive that You will grant it to me. I submit to the person of the Holy Spirit to work this love in me and through me to all others. I deeply desire the true humility of heart necessary and ask You to work this in me. I also submit to the principles in Your Word for this unity to be effective. Please, God, convict me by Your Spirit if in thought, word or deed I am bringing disunity in Your Body now or at any other time. I promise You repentance and restitution wherever You show me. In the name of the Lord Jesus Christ, Amen.

Joy Dawson's Bible-teaching ministry and missionary journeys have taken her to 55 countries on every continent. Most of her teaching ministry has been at spiritual leadership conferences. Multitudes have been blessed by her television and radio ministries, and countless lives have been changed through the international distribution of her CDs and DVDs. The character and ways of God are the biblical basis of her penetrating teachings, which cross denominational lines.

Joy Dawson is the author of three bestselling books,

Intimate Friendship with God
Intercession, Thrilling and Fulfilling
Forever Ruined for the Ordinary

as well as

Some of the Ways of God in Healing
Influencing Children to Become World Changers
The Fire of God
Jesus the Model

Joy and her beloved husband, Jim, served together as unsalaried missionaries with Youth With A Mission, an interdenominational missionary organization operating in nearly 200 countries, and as elders of The Church On The Way, in Van Nuys, California. Joy continues alone in both of these capacities. On February 24, 2013, at 90 years of age Jim went to be with his Lord and Master, to whom he was so devoted. Jim and Joy had 65 years together of a very fulfilling close partnership. Three generations of their family are in full-time ministry in four countries on three different continents. Joy continues to write and teach, as the Lord directs and enables her.